YOU ARE LOVED
AND
YOU ARE NEEDED

*"Faith begins
where human strength ends."*

Jack Wheadon

Warning: This story can change your life!

Warning before you read

Before you dive into this book, a quick warning: you might get mad at me. Not "slightly irritated because someone ate your yogurt" mad. I mean the kind of mad where you start arguing with the pages like they owe you money. At some point you may even feel the holy urge to yeet this book across the room. If that moment comes, please look around first. I refuse to be blamed for a shattered lamp, a traumatized cat, or a spouse walking in and asking, "Why are you fighting literature?"

And if you're reading this on a Kindle, be extra careful. Those things have corners. They travel. They strike. I'm not funding your emergency room visit.

I'll be honest: some of what I say here is intense. But let's face it, Jesus and the apostles weren't exactly strolling around handing out smoothies and inspirational coupons. They said things that made people gasp, argue, repent, or sprint in the opposite direction. I'm simply honoring a long, noble tradition of making readers uncomfortable enough to grow.

My goal isn't to entertain you or tuck you into a warm spiritual blanket. I'm aiming straight for your heart, the part that still twitches when truth pokes it with a stick. If you have even the faintest spiritual pulse, something in these pages will annoy you, inspire you, wake you up, or make you mutter, "Oh no... he's right."

If that happens, congratulations. You're alive. Now let's see what you do with that inconvenient fact.

DEDICATION

*To my family, grandchildren,
and future generations,
especially my wife Wendy,
whose love and faith have
sustained me through every storm.*

You Are Loved and You Are Needed

Copyright © 2025 Pipboxers LLC. All rights reserved.

Title: You Are Loved and You Are Needed
Author: Jack Wheadon
Edition: First
Publication Date: November 2025
ISBN: 9798273211964 (PB)

No part of this publication may be reproduced, stored in a retrieval system, or transmitted in any form or by any means, electronic, mechanical, photocopying, recording, or otherwise, without the prior written permission of the author, except for brief quotations used in reviews or critical articles.

This book is a true account of personal experiences, written to encourage and inspire. Some names and identifying details have been changed to protect individual privacy.

All Scripture quotations are taken from the World English Bible (WEB), which is in the public domain. In certain instances, verses have been paraphrased or adapted for clarity and emotional depth, while maintaining fidelity to the original message of the text.

Publisher:
Pipboxers LLC – Independent Publishing

Printed in the United States of America
First Edition — November 2025

For permissions, correspondence, or reader feedback,

please contact: support@pipboxers.com

Copyright © 2025 Pipboxers LLC. All rights reserved.

ACKNOWLEDGMENTS

I am deeply grateful to all who have walked this path by my side. To my family, my friends, and my brothers and sisters in faith, I thank you for believing in redemption, even when hope seemed to fade.

The pencil sketches contained in this book were created in creative collaboration with the tool ChatGPT (OpenAI). Thanks to this support, it was possible to transform my ideas and photographs into realistic, artistic illustrations.

With gratitude, I remember the technological assistance that brought my vision for this publication to life.

This edition was translated with the help of artificial intelligence, which means that minor linguistic inconsistencies cannot be completely ruled out.

FOREWORD

By Wendy (a proud wife)

This book has been a labor of love that began over 10+ years ago. I'm super proud that Jacek [Jack] has finally finished and published his first-ever book!

It's all about God's perfect timing!

This autobiography is an easy read, and you will not want to put it down! It's full of God-adventures and spiritual nuggets to fuel us on our own spiritual journey, with a good sprinkling of humor. Wherever you are on your path of faith you'll be encouraged, by Jacek's childlike faith and boldness.

I can vouch for him that these are not make-believe stories, but true life adventures with a loving God who has a plan and purpose for each one of us. We just need to surrender!

As I was approaching the end of his book I kept hearing this phrase, "Let Faith Arise "!"

That is my prayer for each person who opens this book that the Holy Spirit will ignite a fire inside of you that no man can quench. Go do amazing things "for" and "with" the Lord ... Greater things are yet to come!!

Love and God's blessings,

FOREWORD

By Klaudia & Isaac

It is a true honor to write the foreword for this remarkable book…one that I finished in less than 24 hours because I simply could not put it down. This story is especially meaningful to me because it is not only a testimony of God's faithfulness, but also my own family's history.

If you are not a Christian, my prayer is that this book encourages you to step out in faith and declare that Jesus is Lord. It is the most important decision you will ever make. Without God, true peace and joy remain out of reach. With Him, even in life's struggles, there is hope, because the ultimate reward is eternal life in His presence. If you are already a Christian, I pray this book strengthens your faith and challenges you to walk boldly, just as the early church did in the book of Acts: healing the sick, casting out demons, and proclaiming the gospel without fear. To be called "crazy about Christ" is, in truth, a great compliment.

My first impression of Jack Wheadon, my father-in-law, is one I will never forget. When I began dating his son Isaac, we traveled from Chicago to Arizona so I could meet his parents. At our very first dinner together, before I was a born-again Christian, Jack looked at me and boldly declared: "I dedicated my son to God, so you better be ready or run!" His words startled me, but they also made me pause and think deeply about what I was stepping into. That moment revealed his boldness and unwavering faith. Looking back, I am profoundly grateful to Jack and Wendy for their prayers for Isaac's future wife long before they knew me, and even more so when Isaac left home at 18 to be with a "pagan, non-practicing Catholic girl."

Their faithfulness and dedication to the Lord changed a generation. Because of their obedience, I met Jesus, and my life was forever transformed.

I will not share my full testimony here…that will be for a book that I need to write inspired by this one but I will say this: what you are about to read is the beginning of a generational story of transformation.

I have been blessed to hear many of these stories firsthand around the dinner table, and they have become treasures to me. As a child, I did not care much for family history, but now I cherish it deeply, especially when I see how God's hand was at work through every detail.

Reading this book has been an honor. It takes courage to sit down, be vulnerable, and write your story for the world to see. This book is not only the Wheadon family's history, it is a testimony of God's faithfulness.

Without giving too much away, I will say this: the journey from a cold, difficult childhood and young adult life marked by poverty and even homelessness, to a life redeemed and transformed by God's grace, is nothing short of extraordinary. Reading it brought me to tears, made me laugh, and filled me with awe at how God carefully pieced each step together.

One moment in particular struck me deeply: the night when despair nearly won, and suicide seemed like the only option. That moment became a turning point, not just for one life, but for generations to come.

Jack, your decision to surrender to Christ not only saved your own life, but also changed the course of our family forever. You planted a seed that continues to bear fruit through your children, grandchildren, and the generations to come. What the enemy meant for evil, God turned into a legacy of faith.

Through you and Wendy, you raised a mighty man of God who knew the truth, and through him, I came to know Jesus. My life was changed, and now I have the privilege of raising your grandchildren to walk in that same truth.

This is the richness of a life in Christ: not measured in money or worldly success, but in the eternal inheritance of knowing the One who truly saves.

I am proud to be a Wheadon. Proud to be your daughter-in-law. And proud to see this story written down so that many more lives may be touched by the testimony of God's goodness.

A few words from Isaac - I can't beat what Klaudia has written. I wholeheartedly agree with her! So, please get ready to read because this book will make you laugh, cry, and reflect, but most of all, it will point you to Jesus. And that is the greatest gift of all.

*****

CONTENTS

1   A World on a Powder Keg............................1

2   Roots and Early Years................................11

3   Fire and Ice..17

4   Between Regimes and Regrets......................25

5   To the Edge of the Bridge............................37

6   A Strange Country and a Stranger..................47

7   Opening the Door to Christmas.....................57

8   The Breaking of Bread................................67

9   Letter of Faith...89

10 Provision and the Red Volvo........................103

11 The Road to Oslo.....................................131

12 Seabourn Pride: A Mission at Sea..................145

13 "Trust in God" Lucy Mable W.......................175

14 From Shame to Testimony...........................193

15 The Woman God Sent................................203

16 From Wounds to Witness............................215

17 Don't Waste Your Last Breath......................225

    Request..233

    Notes & References...................................235

    About The Author.....................................237

Chapter 1

A World On A Powder Keg

Why I chose to write this now?

M Y DEAR GRANDCHILDREN, FAMILY, FRIENDS, and anyone else reading this book. I've decided to write DOWN my story before the Second Civil War in America and before World War III.

I don't know whether you're reading this during those events or after, but I believe you'll want to know what I had to say about the time I lived in the United States.

As I am writing this, 2025 is coming to the end.

It feels as though the entire world is sitting on a powder keg, waiting for a single spark to blow us into oblivion.

Currently, there are 56 armed conflicts raging across the globe.

The United Nations was established after World War II to prevent future wars. Eighty years later, this ineffective organization is grappling with those same 56 conflicts, where millions have died and continue to die every day.

Peace, dialogue, and diplomacy no longer have the power to persuade or prevail.

I want to describe the times I've lived through and what my eyes have seen. The world has gone mad. Let me share what people have been involved in since the first decade of this millennium.

I quote the alleged words of Jacques Attali. I've just begun reading his book A Brief History of the Future, and perhaps I'll have time to write more about it later.

> *"The future will be about finding a way to reduce the population. Of course, we won't be able to execute people or build camps. We'll get rid of them by making them believe it's for their own good. We'll find or provoke something, a pandemic targeted at specific groups, a real economic crisis, a virus affecting the elderly, it doesn't matter. The fearful and the weak will succumb. The foolish will believe and beg for treatment. We'll take care of it, because we'll have the cure that will be the solution. The selection of idiots will happen on its own. They'll walk themselves to the slaughter."*

I must note that Jacques Attali wrote about the concept of humans becoming transhumanist *"mobile devices,"* particularly in his book "A Brief History of the Future, published in 2006.

When he wrote about people as *"mobile devices,"* he wasn't referring to phones, but to human beings themselves, individuals who would carry technology within their bodies (such as chips, sensors, or micro-implants), remain constantly connected to the network, monitored, tracked, and analyzed, and transmit personal data about their health, emotions, opinions, movements, and purchases.

In a sense, they would become part of an information system, like walking smartphones.

In it, he predicts that humanity is heading toward a stage where people will be fully surveilled, subject to both external and self-monitoring, and that the future belongs to *"nomads and altruistic trans-humans,"* mobile individuals enhanced by technology.

According to some sources,

> *"by 2050 we may see the full digitization of human identity, and around 2025, the implantation of microchips in people is expected."*

This is already happening today; one can implant a chip that allows for cashless payments. It's also worth mentioning that many reports from governmental and non-governmental organizations suggest that key global events are expected between 2025 and 2035.

> *"Before 2025, restrictions on mobility and civil liberties are predicted. And in 2025, widespread social uprisings are expected".*

These things were predicted before 2020. In 2020, the entire planet was struck by the COVID-19 pandemic.

The media and globalists, those who seek to eliminate borders and create a totalitarian system modeled after China, even aiming to reduce the world's population to 500 million, unleashed global panic.

The virus appeared suddenly, instilling fear, and people began begging for help and for a vaccine.

They didn't know the vaccine had already been prepared. It turned out the vaccine didn't protect against the virus but contained complex substances that affected women's fertility and men's potency and many other complications.

In the following years, a rise in miscarriages was discovered. Men, instead of protecting their families, began taking hormones to transform into women. They began competing in women's sports, winning against women, even though they never were and never will be women.

Young men today have testosterone levels comparable to those typically found in fifty-year-old men. Diet is the problem.

The media, press and television, mostly report only what suits their sponsors. People lost trust in official sources and began creating independent news channels.

I do not know if you have heard of someone named Isaiah, but he said something very fitting:

> "Woe to those who call evil good, and good evil…"
>
> (Isaiah 5:20, WEB, excerpt)

And Paul, formerly Saul, wrote in his letter to the Romans during the Roman Empire words that fit our times perfectly:

> "Since they no longer saw fit to acknowledge God, He let them go their own way. And everything began to unravel: evil spread, greed flourished, betrayal became normal. They turned life on earth into a kind of hell, envy, murder, conflict, deception. Look at them: malicious, venomous, hypocritical blasphemers. Bullies, braggarts, relentless talkers. Always inventing new ways to destroy what's good. They abandon their parents when they become inconvenient. Foolish, cruel, heartless, and cold. And it's not that they don't know better — they know exactly what they're doing. They spit in God's face. And worse, they applaud those who sin most boldly."
>
> (Author's paraphrase on Romans 1:28–32, WEB)

Society has become divided. Some stand on one side, others on the opposite. The family, the smallest unit of society, is under constant attack from leftist ideologies.

Young people have stopped believing in the institution of marriage.

They live as we say colloquially, "playing house," and women raise children alone, often with financial benefits because the state supports their situation.

Young boys, deprived of fathers, seek role models in gangs, often under pressure or out of desperation. They do not know that a righteous father raises children in the fear of God, as Scripture says:

> "Train up a child in the way he should go, and when he is old he will not depart from it." (Proverbs 22:6, WEB)

> "Unless Yahweh builds the house, they who build it labor in vain. Unless Yahweh watches over the city, the watchman guards it in vain." (Psalm 127:1, WEB)

In the USA, although black male citizens make up about 6% of the population, they commit over 50%, and according to some sources, even 75% of the most serious crimes. Prisons are filled with young men without fathers who should show them how to be heads of households and role models for the next generation.

Deceived by society and the media, they learn in prison how to become more effective criminals. Driven by greed, they don't realize:

> "For the love of money is a root of all kinds of evil. Some have been led astray from the faith in their greed and have pierced themselves through with many sorrows." (1 Timothy 6:10, WEB)

And:

> "Where there is no revelation, the people cast off restraint; but one who keeps the law is blessed." (Proverbs 29:18, WEB)

In 2020, the elections were considered fraudulent by many American citizens. Surely, matters that were once dismissed as conspiracies will eventually come to light, yet from what I can see, all such accusations are turning out to be true.

The southern border was opened, and over 20 million illegal immigrants entered the country, including individuals released from prisons, correctional facilities, and psychiatric hospitals.

In so-called *"sanctuary cities,"* they commit crimes, and politicians, mainly Democrats, celebrate the potential of new voters.

City budgets are collapsing, while illegal immigrants receive Social Security numbers, cash for shopping, and other benefits, just to vote for the Democratic Party.

After the 2024 elections, Republicans came to power with President Donald Trump at the helm. Deportations of illegal immigrants began, especially of criminals. Scenes of chaos unfold in many cities. Those who fulfill their duties are labeled *"Gestapo," "fascists," "Nazis."*

On September 10, 2025, in front of thousands of witnesses, a 31-year-old man, Charlie Kirk, was murdered.

He preached about Jesus and urged young people on university campuses to choose dialogue over violence, to sit at the table and discuss the problems of the country and the world.

An investigation is underway, and it may reveal that the accused is not the actual perpetrator, in my humble opinion.

It begs us to quote the writer named Matthew, who recorded the words of the greatest Speaker the world has ever known. Jesus said:

> "Blessed are those who have been persecuted for righteousness' sake, for theirs is the Kingdom of Heaven." (Matthew 5:10, WEB)

Additionally, the USA had a black president, Barack Hussein Obama, from 2008 to 2016. According to many sources, his wife Michelle may be biologically male, named Mike.

In France, the president is Emmanuel Macron, and according to some reports, his wife may also be male.

I wonder why the leaders of such powerful countries lie to their citizens straight to their faces, pretending to be someone they are not, presenting themselves as legitimate, upright individuals.

I don't know if the world has reached the end of its madness or if this is just the beginning of insanity.

Since February 24, 2022, war has raged between Russia and Ukraine. Poland, (as Ukraine's neighbor and a NATO member), could be drawn into a conflict worse than World War II. It is frightening to think that the words of Jesus in Matthew 24 may be unfolding before our eyes:

> "You will hear of wars and rumors of wars. See that you aren't troubled, for all this must happen, but the end is not yet. For nation will rise against nation, and kingdom against kingdom." (Matthew 24:6–7, WEB)

In October 2025, the UN and countries like the UK, France, and others, except the USA, announced the recognition of the State of Palestine. I don't know what will come of it.

On October 7th, 2023, the terrorist organization Hamas launched a brutal invasion of Israeli border villages, murdering approximately 1,200 Jewish civilians and festival attendees in cold blood. The horror of that day was captured on bodycams, cell phones, and security footage a 43-minute compilation assembled by the Israeli military.

Though never released to the public, this footage was shown privately to journalists and officials. Those who viewed it reportedly required psychiatric support afterward. The images were so graphic, so inhuman, that even seasoned war correspondents were shaken.

It was not just a massacre, it was a glimpse into the darkest corners of human depravity. In September 2025, Prime Minister Keir Starmer announced the implementation of a national Digital ID system, to be fully deployed by the end of the current parliamentary term, no later than August 2029.

Countries that have already introduced digital ID systems include Singapore, India, Austria, China, Bosnia and Herzegovina, Nigeria, Pakistan, and of course, the European Union.

To that list we must now add Estonia, known for its advanced e-government infrastructure; South Korea, where digital IDs are integrated with mobile services; Kenya, which launched Huduma Namba; Brazil, with its national digital registry; and the Philippines, which rolled out PhilSys to unify citizen records.

Step by step, the world is moving forward, not toward empowerment, but toward the subjugation of humanity, just as the so-called wise men of this world have predicted.

The world has gone mad!

I do not want to say it is like the days of Noah, but if it is, then this may be a profoundly biblical moment. And soon, something may happen that the entire world will be talking about.

Be sure to read chapter 24 of the Gospel of Matthew, because Jesus Himself said:

> "As the days of Noah were, so will be the coming of the Son of Man." (Matthew 24:37, WEB)

> "Watch therefore, for you don't know in what hour your Lord comes." (Matthew 24:42, WEB)

I know, it sounds like crazy times, but I pray and hope that I am wrong about this prediction.

Unfortunately, I do NOT see anything positive ahead of us but only more hate, division, and disaster.

* * *

After this truly short apocalyptic entrance I would like to tell you that this is not going to be a few pages booklet because I'm not smart enough to summarize everything in such a short format. Instead, this will be a journey, giving you a glimpse into my life.

Another reason I began drafting this book is that I never had the chance to ask my grandparents about their lives and what they went through, and I cannot find any materials that would give me insight into their struggles and successes.

At the end of the day, (if you are my family) my life story is your history, your roots. I want to take you on a journey that I hope, believe, and pray will positively impact your life.

Please forgive my limited vocabulary. I am not hiding anything. English was the last language I learned.

And yes, I did not make a mistake; I did not learn English in school. But more on that soon in my story. Brace yourselves, this will take some time for you to discover.

I hope this will not be boring. The only thing I would like to add is a warning: *"I am a very dangerous person."*

What you are about to hear will have a tremendous impact on your future. I owe you that sentence. After you read what I have written, you'll never be able to say:

"I didn't know…"

OK, let's begin!

* * * * *

Chapter 2

Roots And Early Years

*My family, my grandmother,
and the faith that would not let go.*

I AM A SIXTY-FOUR year old straight, white male, and I have been grateful for every day especially since my heart attack at the age of fifty-four. My goal is not to be wealthy or famous but to be found faithful to the task I received when I was twenty-eight years old. I know you are thinking, *"What are you talking about?"* Well, you will learn soon enough.

Now, I will try to tell you what I remember about my grandparents and paint a picture of my surroundings. On my mother's side, I only knew her mother, Wanda Olejniczak, who was my grandmother.

I visually remember my great-grandmother, though I do not recall her name. She lived with my grandma's sister Gertruda.

I remember these family members, because sometimes we were visiting them to watch a TV program in black and white, on only one channel.

It was around 1967. They were the only family who had a television at home.

As for my grandfather, I never met him. He died before I was born. My grandmother told me that he was in Gross-Rosen, a Nazi German concentration camp. I do not know how he ended up back with his family, but when he returned, he was extremely sick, weighing only about 30–40 kg (66–88 lbs.).

He had been starved nearly to death by the Nazi Germans. She said he would eat with his eyes, desperate for food. In poor health, one day he ate too much, which caused a volvulus (a twisting of the intestines), and he knew he was going to die soon. He asked his family to gather so he could say goodbye, and he passed away in bed in front of his wife and children.

My grandmother became a widow at 33, with four children: Leonard, Stefan, Gertruda, and Włodzimierz. She never remarried and devoted her life to raising her children until she died at the age 91 if I remember correctly.

She was a devoted believer, and I can only imagine that her faith in God helped her get through the tough times, especially after losing her husband.

I was her first grandson, the first son of her only daughter. I will write a few more words about this statement later. There was a time when Grandma Wanda lived with us in our apartment, helping because both of my parents worked.

My father was a professional soldier in the Polish Army, and my mother worked as a bartender in a bar near the railway station in Ostrów Wielkopolski.

I remember this well because I often visited her at work. As a child, I liked visiting her there because there was always plenty of food, desserts, and soda.

My father worked nearby at the military base. I remember hearing the story of how my parents met.

After my father finished his work at the base, he went to the bar for a beer where my mom worked.

One day, a man in line could not pay for his drink, but he wanted it so badly that he took out his glass eye and handed it to my "future" mother across the counter. Instead of being shocked like most people would, my young, beautiful mother calmly took the glass eye, placed it in the beer glass, and said, "OK, you can pay me tomorrow."

When my father saw this, he was astonished and realized she was something special, so he asked her out.

At least, that is the story I remember of how my parents met for the first time.

I have two younger sisters, Małgorzata and Anna.

When I was about 7 years old in 1968, and we lived on the 5th floor of a military apartment building. Yes, the 5th floor (ground floor plus four levels) without an elevator.

When we returned from the store with groceries, we would shout for someone at home to lower a rope from our balcony so we could pull up the groceries instead of carrying them up all those stairs. That saved us many trips!

Now, I'd have a heart attack going up and down those stairs, or maybe I'd be in better shape. I also remember how we used the rope to lower our father's military bags when he left for war with Czechoslovakia in 1968. We did not know if we'd ever see him again. It was an exceedingly difficult time for our family.

My grandmother Wanda, a widow herself, saw her only daughter with three small children and feared history might repeat itself. It was a dramatic time.

One funny but painful memory of Grandma stands out. We were heading to the city and about to catch the bus.

My grandmother, eager to hurry me along, swung her purse at me to give me a push on the butt, but at that moment, I turned around.

Instead of hitting my backside, she accidentally hit me square in the face.

I covered my mouth in pain, and when she realized how serious it was, she saw that she'd knocked out my four front teeth! It's funny how after half a century, I can still remember that incident.

Another funny memory comes to mind as well. When we lived in an apartment complex, I went to a small store to buy croissants. As I waited in line, when it was my turn, I suddenly forgot the name of the product I wanted. I stood there, frozen, unable to speak. People were in a hurry, waiting behind me, and I panicked. Out of nowhere, the name "*Carol*" popped into my head *(I have no idea why)*. But a croissant in Polish is called "rogal."

Finally, I pointed to the croissants in the display case, and the shopkeeper handed me a few. I was so flustered that I forgot where I was, and I started crying. A woman saw me crying and asked why. I told her I'd forgotten where I lived, but I managed to explain I lived in military apartments, and she pointed me in the right direction. I found my way back home after all.

These silly childhood moments stick with us, but they're innocent and insignificant in the grand scheme of things.

Because my father was in the Polish Army, he was never comfortable with Roman Catholic traditions, quietly introduced and encouraged by my grandmother in our home.

I didn't know my father didn't believe in God because I'd seen wedding pictures of him and my mom in a church, so I assumed he must have been a believer. But as a child, I noticed his strong opposition to both the Roman Catholic Church and God.

I went through First Communion and Confirmation, but by age 15, I was practically an atheist like my father.

We didn't have a great relationship, but somehow, I started to develop a deep dislike for the Roman Catholic Church and the whole concept of God.

Instead of attending church on Sundays, I would go to a coffee shop across the street to find out when mass would end, so I could time my return home perfectly.

My mother, under my father's influence, also stopped attending church regularly.

Our loving grandmother was the driving force behind our religious practices, but it just didn't appeal to me as a teenager.

At 16, I was kicked out of religious education class because I kept asking difficult questions and challenging the priest. He couldn't stand my arrogance, so I was removed.

Since my parents didn't care much about my religious education, nothing happened as a result. This only deepened my belief that God didn't exist, and I grew more convinced that religion was man-made idea. To me, God was a human invention. A way for the sick, poor, and desperate to find hope.

When I stood inside the church, gazing at the paintings and figurines, I watched them closely, half expecting one of the figures to wink at me. Maybe then I would have believed. But it never happened.

I observed people lining up to kiss the feet of statues of Jesus, Mary, the holy apostles, and other saints. I couldn't make sense of it. These were man-made objects, purchased, cast from plaster, painted or carved.

For a young person like me, it was something confusing, something difficult to accept. The idea of believing in God the Creator simply disappeared from my life. Since I no longer believed in God, I thought there were no consequences for my actions beyond this life.

Heaven and hell were just stories, so who cared what we did while we were alive? Right?!?

* * * * *

Chapter 3

Fire And Ice

*My father's war scars,
and the war that entered our home.*

N OW, I FEEL I MUST start talking about my father. He was born in 1937 in Honoratówka, near Lviv, during a time when Poland was going through troubled times. Being situated between Germany and Russia, Poland did not have the best neighbors.

I remember my father sharing his past with us, but when we were young, we didn't pay much attention to these stories. We were young and foolish, and we didn't appreciate the history of our forefathers. Now, I see the importance of knowing these facts, but it took me half a century to realize it.

So, my father was born in what is now Ukraine. When I was 15, we were invited to a wedding and traveled as a family to Ukraine to see where my father was born.

He showed us the places where he spent his childhood.

The most dramatic part of the trip was when he told us about his two older brothers.

One day, Ukrainians turned against their Polish neighbors and started killing them without hesitation. I recently discovered that a movie was made about this terrible time, titled "*Wołyń*". In English, it's called "Hatred".

My sister Anna watched this film in the cinema and encouraged me to see it. I've watched it three times at home. My wife couldn't gather the courage to watch it with me. Many years later, I received a copy of a book that mentioned how my father's two brothers were killed during this time. Jozef was 21 and Stanislaw was 20 years old. They were burned alive in a shed.

My father told me that as a child, he lived in a dugout and could only go out at night so no one would see him. He used to point to the scar on his left cheek and explain that one day; while going to the doghouse, the dog attacked him, biting his cheek. He slept in trees and dugouts and lacked the peaceful, loving environment that many children have. He grew up in survival mode. I remember him saying, *"Only the strongest survive."*

Life, to him, wasn't a greenhouse, warm and cozy, it was tough, and those conditions prepared him for survival. Now I understand that he wanted the best for us. He wanted us to be tough and strong, just like he had to be, having grown up during World War II. Of course, we were from a different era.

We hadn't seen or heard of such horrors. We grew up with the assurance that our "*brother*" Russia would defend us from the Germans, and we wouldn't have to worry about another world war.

My father, being a soldier, was accustomed to a strict lifestyle. He couldn't stand seeing his children playing instead of doing something productive. Since he hadn't had a playful childhood, he didn't think we needed one either.

His cold upbringing caused friction between my mother's family, her three brothers, and my grandmother. There were disagreements. I don't know what they were about, but my parents had a plot of land to build a house, and it happened to be located between my mother's brothers. We became neighbors, and as children, we were stuck between the hammer and the anvil. My parents didn't talk to the family, but we still wanted to play with our cousins. It was a crazy time.

My father treated me like his young soldier. I don't recall hearing *"I love you" or "I'm proud of you."* He was always yelling, telling me I couldn't "drive a nail in the sand." It sounds silly, but that's how I grew up.

You should know that I could play classical guitar in the school orchestra, play the piano, and recite poems publicly at school.

But somehow this wasn't enough for my father. I understand him today; he wanted me to be like Rambo, ready to defeat the enemy. But we were living in a different era, long after World War II.

I've never shared this publicly, but I think now is the time. When I was 15 or 16, we were building our new house, and I remember my father would take me straight from school to work on it. The way he spoke to me, or rather, shouted, made me so angry. One day, we were preparing the first floor for pouring concrete. I remember it like it was yesterday.

He was kneeling, crushing old bricks and stones on the floor with a hammer, and I was standing nearby with an ax. In that moment, an intense hatred for him overtook me, and I almost committed an unspeakable crime. I almost struck my father. But somehow, something, or someone, stopped me.

I remember planning to quarter my father's body and throw it into the sewage tank. That would have been the end of my life too. Imagine such a scenario: my father survived the genocide of Poles and Jews at the hands of Ukrainians in 1943, only to be killed by his own son in his own home.

Well, if there's no God, there are no consequences for our actions after death. If there's no God, why would this act be immoral?

Where did the moral code come from? Who came up with this morality code? How to explain this kind of evil?

Where does this come from? If there is no God, who created supposedly everything good, who created evil?

My parents didn't teach me to be evil. I didn't take lessons on how to be good or bad. Maybe morality is within us or maybe not. But I will say more about this later. Be patient please.

Returning to my father's story, I recently discovered that after the terrible time when his two brothers were murdered, he fled with the rest of his family to western Poland. At some point, they changed their surname from Mojsej to Mojsiejów.

My sister, who had some contact with Polish Jews in Israel, learned that "*Mojsej*" means "*Moses*," and "*Mojsiejów*" means "*descendant of Moses*." It seems they may have changed their name, and perhaps even their faith, just to survive those terrible times.

Today, I understand that my father wanted good things for me and my sisters, but he was handicapped by his difficult childhood.

He was unable to give the love that a normal father might have given. You can't give what you don't have. I remember swearing that I would never be like my father.

I promised myself I'd be the opposite of him, that he would be the anti-example for my life. Let's fast forward a bit.

On my 18th birthday, I came home from school. My father was sitting under the stairs, drinking wine with a neighbor. I greeted him and said:

"Do you know it's my 18th birthday today?"

He replied,

"So what? Go work in a bar, everyone has one, even pigs have birthdays."

I remember the first birthday cake I ever had was on my 30th birthday. It was also the day I married Wendy. Because of my upbringing, birthdays aren't a big deal to me.

I have to remind myself that the people around me grew up in an atmosphere of love, and I need to adjust my thinking and celebrate with them the day they were born into this world.

It seems my father's view on birthdays was:

"So what? Everyone has one."

I laugh now as I recall this, but it took me decades to calm down about it. My emotions have cooled, and I can talk about it without much drama today.

I forgot to mention that I went to a technical catering school, where I learned all about cooking, including the chemical and physical processes involved. I preferred spending time in the kitchen rather than under the car with my father, who was always fixing his German car.

I couldn't stand how he shouted:

"Bring me this, bring me that, you moron, don't you know what a tool is that I need?"

So, I chose the kitchen. It was warm and there was access to food.

After technical high school, I decided I wanted to continue my education. I wanted to go to a big city, Poznań, and study at the Agricultural Academy and continue my profession.

From the age of 16, I had a passion for learning languages. I learned Russian, German, Spanish, and French. Back then, I didn't care for English, I didn't like the London accent; it sounded unnatural to me.

Who would have thought that I'd end up speaking English every day? And I never even learned it in school! But more on that later.

I spoke French for many hours every day, preparing for the exam after graduating from technical school.

I went with a friend to Poznań to take the entrance exam, but unfortunately, I didn't pass and wasn't admitted to the Agricultural Academy.

I returned home. Before that, my mother's brother Wlodek and his wife Zdzisia offered to help me prepare for the entrance exams the following year. In the meantime, they suggested I find a job to pay for private lessons.

Excited by the idea, I returned to my parents, ready to leave my hometown and venture out into the big world. However, there was a problem. My father had built a house, and in this large house, he'd designated a section as a bar, a kind of pub.

From the age of 16, I worked there every day after school. My mother would prepare dinner, and I'd work in our bar. My idea of leaving home and continuing my studies didn't align with my father's plan. He wanted me to work for him in the bar. In his mind, there was no other option.

And now, his 18-year-old son had the audacity to decide to leave and do what he wanted to do. My father became furious. I was afraid to leave my room. I had only two singles to listen to on my record player: Bicycle by Freddie Mercury and Beethoven's 5th Symphony.

I remember it like it was yesterday. After hours of shouting, he stormed into my room, looked at me, and yelled:

"You're a piece of sh*t, not even worth touching!"

Then he destroyed my entire room. Everything was flying in the air, but I didn't move.

I just sat in my armchair in the middle of my bedroom, waiting for my certain death. When he finally left my room, my mind was empty. Everything felt weightless. I didn't know what had just happened.

I didn't leave the room for a few hours. I read my French books, too afraid to think.

After a few hours, my father came back and started packing his clothes. My mother asked him what he was doing. He said he was moving out of the house. He declared that two lions couldn't share the same territory.

When I heard that my father couldn't stay in the same place as me, I quickly packed my books and a small plastic bag of clothes. Back then, I had more books than clothes.

I left my room, approached him, and asked if I could say goodbye, as I was leaving the house under these circumstances.

Her replied:

"No, you cannot say goodbye."

I then went to my mother and asked her the same thing. Honestly, I don't remember her answer.

Of course, I hugged my two crying younger sisters Anna and Malgorzata and I left my home with only equivalent of $1 in my pocket, never to return there to live again.

* * * * *

Chapter 4

Between Regimes And Regrets

Communism, Solidarity, and the long road to manhood.

I WENT TO MY GRANDMOTHER and uncle, who was taking care of her. They couldn't believe what had happened, but they immediately helped me move to Poznań, where I could live with another uncle and his wife. This was in July 1980. That was the beginning of my adult life. What a drama.

I remember 30 years later, when my son Isaac, 18 years old, wanted to leave our house in Arizona and move to Chicago, Illinois, 1,800 miles away, because he was in love with his now-wife, Klaudia.

The moment he said that he was going to move to Chicago, the black-and-white movie of my summer in 1980 played in front of my eyes. I gave him my blessing to go wherever he wanted. I didn't want my child to experience the same horror I did. I'll need to spend many hours telling you about the beginning of my adult life, but maybe I'll find time for that later.

> [My dear reader, if you are still young, you probably lack patience, but I can't know for sure because I can't hear or see you.

I suggest putting this book on the side and coming back later because this is just the beginning. When you cool down, sit comfortably and continue. I guarantee you won't fall asleep. And if you do, sorry but I am sure you will not.]

I should mention that I was quite active in my technical school, and at 18 years old, I was able to join the Communist Party. If you are my offspring, you will probably say:

"Are you serious? You were a member of that party?"

Well, my dear grandchildren, friends and everybody else who is reading this book, when you're young, you lack knowledge. You're usually rebellious. You think you know everything, and then you make stupid decisions. Your ears are blocked to the wisdom that is screaming at you, but you are simply deaf, your ego dominates everything and you and I in this situation make big mistakes.

Yes, I joined the Communist Party because I knew that if you weren't with those in power, achieving your goals would be nearly impossible. Poland and other countries in the Warsaw Pact were corrupt to the bone.

Only those with connections could get what they wanted. I learned this from my mother, who could get building materials when they were impossible to buy, simply because she knew people and she knew how to deal with them.

I know that the book, *"The Art of the Deal"* was not written yet, but my mother could be an early writer of this bestseller. That was a priceless lesson for me: to have connections.

Now I was in a big city where I knew no one. My life was like a clean slate. My uncle was a musician, so I often saw him perform at the Poznań Philharmonic Symphony.

Freedom from my parents, but still under family supervision. It was a different story.

CHAPTER 4 - BETWEEN REGIMES AND REGRETS

My uncle was puzzled when he received a letter from my father, who said that when he came to Poznań, he would demolish their front door with an ax. He was furious that they were helping me make my way in this big city.

You probably don't understand, but in those days, Polish people didn't trust people from areas where many Ukrainians lived. They were somewhat xenophobic, and they saw my father as different, a soldier, possibly even a killer. They feared he might harm them for helping me.

Imagine my feelings towards my father. Any tender feelings I might have had simply didn't exist any longer. I knew I had to do something with my life to free these people from my father's anger.

I moved and started staying with Andrew, a friend from technical school, for a while, and continued taking lessons to prepare for the next year's entry exams to the Agricultural Academy. Well, life is full of surprises. There was a saying in those days, especially in small towns like mine: "Do you think they're waiting for you at the Hotel Polonez?"

This was the number one hotel in the city. Once again, connections: my aunt knew someone who knew someone in charge of the hotel, and I got an interview there.

I applied for a job as a waiter in this posh hotel, and because I had finished culinary school and spoke besides Polish, also Russian, German, and French, I got the job.

My family was probably shocked that I managed what seemed almost impossible. Soon after, Poland was going through hell, Solidarity started demonstrating against the Communist regime.

I did not tell anyone I was a member of the Communist Party after I saw what they were doing to members of Solidarity.

They'd arrest people at night, strip them naked, pour cold water on them in the winter, beat them with rubber batons, drive them to the middle of nowhere, and leave them.

I realized the Communists were bad, really bad, and I wanted nothing more to do with them. I destroyed my Communist Party ID and joined Solidarity. My anger towards the regime grew, and I no longer wanted to live in a country like that.

I had learned other languages, so I knew it was only a matter of time before I left. Hold on, there's a catch. If you were a man, you had to serve two years in the military before you could get a passport. And after you returned from any trip abroad, you had to give your passport back to the authorities. If you were late, you'd be in serious trouble.

For those who think Socialism and Communism are wonderful ideas, I'm telling you from my experience that you're so misguided that even a doctor couldn't help you. If you're offended by that, I'm glad, it means you read what I said. If you're my grandchild leaning toward the left side of the political spectrum, I'm probably spinning in my grave if I am already dead. May God have mercy on you, because if I were around, I'd make sure that foolishness was wiped from your mind.

Now, imagine this: I failed the exam again for the Agricultural Academy. I won't go into why. But I decided to go to the authorities and tell them I wanted to do my two years of mandatory military service.

Imagine the officer's reaction when he learned my father was a major in the Polish Army and that I wanted to serve without hesitation. He asked:

> *"Can't your father pull some strings to excuse you from service?"*

I said:

> *"Absolutely No, I want to serve and then be free to go if possible."*

They asked if I wanted to be a corporal or a waiter during my service. I said:

> "I don't care. What do you think you're going to teach me?"

It sounds arrogant, but I told them,

> "I've been driving a jeep since I was 14. I did my homework on military base. I've never had long hair. I've never worn jeans because my father hated Western fashion. I know how to clean my shoes, iron my clothes, and maintain a weapon. What do you want me to learn?"

Well, since my education was above average, they sent me to military school to become a corporal. It was a brutal experience, but of course, I made it through. A few weeks ago, I shared this story with someone, so I'll share it with you, too.

I had a golden medallion given to me by a friend, and one of the corporals who trained us badly wanted to buy it. I always told him, *"I'm not selling it."* He wasn't happy about that.

A quick digression: since I was 15, I had been into martial arts. I had friends who taught me some moves in karate and kung fu.

One night, the corporal called me over again and asked about the medallion. When I said no, he gave me a brutal task: polish a 100-yard corridor with a weighted mop. It was exhausting.

After I finished, he called me to his room and asked again about the medallion. This time, my response was different. Tears filled my eyes, and with holy indignation boiling in me, I said:

> "I won't give you or sell you this medallion. But I promise you, when I finish my military service, I'll find you and kill you."

You may say"

> "Grandpa, you were a bad-ass!"

Well, it seems I had something in my eyes that made this man, who was bigger than me, shocked by my reply.

He apologized for what he had done. That's an event I remember vividly, even after almost half a century.

There's a movie called *"Fala"* on You Tube that will give you an idea of what I went through. It is in Polish but maybe you will find with your language subtitles to understand what I am writing about.

After two months, we had the army swearing-in day, on December 13, 1981. I was working in the officers' casino on December 12th, and I returned to the barracks at 3:00 AM (already December 13th), exhausted after preparing the casino for guests. At 4:00 AM, I was jolted awake by my corporal screaming that there was an alarm. I responded,

"Sorry guys, I just got back from working at the officers' casino, and I need to sleep."

They quickly told me this wasn't a drill, it was a Martial Law alarm, a war alert! I didn't fully understand what it meant, but by looking at the faces of the older soldiers, I realized this was different from the usual alerts.

I was the only soldier out of 600 men who had no one visit me during the swearing-in ceremony. But, as they say, "Every pig has its birthday," so I wasn't too bothered about my family not being there to celebrate with me.

I went to work as usual. When my captain saw me at the casino, he asked:

"What the hell are you doing here, soldier?"

I replied, *"I'm working, Captain."* He said, *"Go to your family."* I answered, *"Nobody came today."*

Feeling sorry for me, he wanted to give me three days off, but due to Martial Law, no one was allowed to leave the military base. Our battalion was responsible for protecting the government in Warsaw.

A few months later, we had a mandatory shooting exam, but I hadn't attended any of the practice sessions because I was working in the officers' casino.

A fellow soldier came to fetch me for the exam, and I told him, *"I'm working in the casino."*

But there was no getting out of it, I had to go. They asked if I knew how to assume a shooting position. I replied, "No."

After showing me how, they handed me five bullets and an AK-47, instructing me to shoot at a target 100 meters away and report my score to the captain. I fired five shots, ran to the target, and reported, "I scored 47 out of 50." The captain looked at me and said:

"What the hell are you doing in the casino? You're one of the best shooters in the battalion."

That marked the end of my time at the casino. The captain took me under his wing and started preparing me for the corporal exam after his work hours. Now, that was something.

A quick side note: Since I didn't have any visitors during my first six months of service and had no money to buy sweets, I donated blood just to get two bars of chocolate. This may seem like a small thing, but I want you, my dear grandchildren, to appreciate what you have in life.

After passing the corporal exam, I was assigned to a military airport security company. Now a corporal, I have many stories to tell from that time, but I need to share something important to set the stage for what came next.

The first time I was in charge, while the professional soldiers were home on leave, I had to ensure the soldiers cleaned their rooms and kept everything in order. It didn't go well.

We had some highlanders who were supposed to finish their mandatory service, but because of Martial Law, they were kept at the base longer.

They were angry, and one of them had just become a father, so they wanted to celebrate. However, alcohol was strictly forbidden on the base.

They held a small, quiet party in the uniform storage room, but when they went to the shower room to get water, they forgot to close the door. That night, the duty officer came to inspect my company. He asked why the light was on, as all soldiers were supposed to be asleep.

I pretended not to know. He opened the door, and there it was, quiet, but a full-on celebration. Everything was laid out on the table.

He grabbed two bottles of vodka, which was all the proof he needed that a violation had occurred. He told me I would be jailed for failing to maintain order in the company. Suddenly, one of the highlanders snatched the bottles of vodka and ran to the bathroom to destroy the evidence.

The officer, a captain I believe, leaped on the soldier's back, trying to grab his own gun. When I saw this, I jumped on the officer's back to stop him from harming my soldier. I probably saved that soldier's life, but I knew I was in deep trouble now.

I understood the regulations, but pulling a gun over two bottles of vodka seemed extreme.

The next morning, after a sleepless night, the captain entered the corridor and didn't even want to hear my report. He immediately called me into his office. I expected to be jailed and was already imagining the story I'd tell my friends. Instead, he asked me:

"Did you know about the highlanders' party?"

I firmly replied, *"No."*

He knew I was lying but seemed to appreciate that I didn't rat out my soldiers. He punished me with 10 consecutive 24-hour guard shifts, to which I gladly said, *"Yes, sir. I accept."*

Inside my mind, I was screaming with joy. I had been expecting jail time, so this was a big relief.

This might not sound like something to brag about, but as a young corporal, I earned immense respect from the older soldiers.

They respected me more than anyone else, and I was just seven months into my service. Soldiers like that are often referred to as "*cats*" young and inexperienced.

The same day I received my penalty, the captain took me to the area where soldiers played table tennis. He pointed out some cigarette butts behind the mattresses and said:

"*Do you see that? This place is dirty.*"

I was amazed that he didn't even have to look closely because he knew that soldiers had been smoking there and tossing their cigarette remains behind the equipment.

The next day, during my first penalty guard shift, I gathered all 140 soldiers and flooded the entire corridor with soapy water. The foam was at least a foot high. I assigned each soldier to clean their area, ensuring everything, floors, walls, even the pictures, were polished to perfection.

The next morning, when the captain arrived, he smelled the fresh scent in the air and asked:

"*What happened?*" I replied, "*You told me the company quarters were dirty, so I made the soldiers clean everything.*"

He was stunned that a soldier with only seven months of service had managed to get everyone to clean like never before.

He called all the corporals to his office and shocked us again.

He demoted the corporal in charge of the second platoon to a squad leader (in charge of just 10 soldiers) and promoted me to platoon leader. I didn't ask for it, but that's what happened.

He then asked me to write something on a piece of paper, and after seeing how well I wrote, he made me his personal scribe.

A year later, I earned my third stripe and became a "lance corporal." The other soldiers resented me because I was climbing the ranks, and they couldn't understand how it was happening. Since I was responsible for training soldiers on security duties at the air force base, they resented me so much that they plotted to beat me up before leaving for home after two years of service.

Now, my dear grandchildren, let me tell you: I was so obsessed with martial arts back then that I used to take a bus twice a week from the base to Poznań to train in Kyokushin karate. On the base, I'd spar with six guys at once, standing in the middle. When the soldiers who planned to attack me saw what I was capable of, they abandoned their plan to harm me.

There's much more I could say, but let's move on.

After my service in the army, I started working at the newest hotel in the city. A few years later, I became a master waiter.

And life went on. I won't go into details, but I noticed at work that my colleagues were aging, still working hard at the hotel.

I started asking myself, what does the future hold for me in this profession? Something had to change; this couldn't go on. But what can you do when you earn the equivalent of $30 a month? I'll skip a few years of meaningless existence, as there's nothing to boast about.

Working hard, spending hard money in the night clubs, it was Sodom and Gomorrah. However, one day, a young, pretty girl came to my section at the hotel. "Okay, Grandpa, remember, Grandma will see what you have written" you'd probably say. Well, she knows all my story.

At the time, I didn't know English, but this young American girl was apparently learning French, since she was from the state of Nebraska.

At the end of her visit, she told me that she didn't have much money with her, but she would come back in the evening and bring me a gift for my service.

Wow, a gift from an American! A storm of thoughts ran through my head, what could it be? Of course, cash is the best gift for a waiter. After all, it's hard to live on $30 a month. In the evening, she returned with her father, and as they walked towards me, she carried a black book in a manner that made it seem like the coronation of the Queen of England was about to take place. In her broken French, she said:

> "This is a gift for you; it's a very important book that has been in our family."

I took it, thanked her, "Merci," and they left.

"Grandpa, did you sell the book to get more money?" you might ask. No, I didn't sell it. I looked at it in the back room and put it in my locker. It was a Bible, in English, with pictures. Since I didn't know English, it lay there for over a year among my things. Life went on.

My desire to leave Poland, make some money and to do something with my life led me to reconnect with Andrew, an old school friend. He helped me arrange legal work in Norway. I got my passport and visa, and I knew these would be my last days in my home country. I said goodbye to my sisters, but I made sure not to raise any suspicions at the border because I knew I wasn't coming back.

Communism is a monster that doesn't want to lose its slaves. The illusion of freedom is only for those in power; the rest are just useful fools.

* * * * *

Chapter 5

To The Edge Of The Bridge

Norway, hunger, and the first voice that saved my life.

I N THE SUMMER OF 1987, I sailed on a ferry to Sweden and then took a train to Norway. Not knowing English but being good in other languages, I arrived at a farm where I worked for about three months, if memory serves me right.

I remember I had directions to find the place where Polish laborers lived, but since it was already night, I couldn't find them. Luckily, someone had left their very small Polish car – Fiat 126 unlocked in front of a huge barn. After several attempts to find an entrance into the building, I gave up and got into the car with my luggage and slept for a few hours. The nights were cold, even in summer, remember, we're talking about northern Norway.

The next day, I was shown what to do and where, and at 5 a.m., I started working on the farm, cutting cauliflowers, Chinese lettuce, cabbage, and so on. When I touched the cauliflowers early in the morning, a layer of frost covered them, and it felt like millions of needles were piercing the pads of my fingers.

When the sun came up, it was the most beautiful moment, as it melted the frost, and the pain in my fingers disappeared.

I spent more time outdoors than ever before in my adult life, and my appetite increased to the point where I could eat an entire loaf of bread for lunch. *"Bread for lunch, Grandpa? That seems odd!"* you might say.

Well, my dears, we were responsible for preparing our own food, so when we went to the store, we looked for the cheapest items. There was always stale bread in the baskets. Bread was very expensive in Norway, but the stale ones were on sale, so for one crown, you could buy a whole loaf. If you knew me, you'd know that Grandpa bought an entire metal cart full of stale bread, so there was plenty of food.

I must add that after a few days, the bread turned green, not because someone painted it, but because mold started to grow. Back then, people weren't poisoned by food like they are now in the USA. Mold could develop. Nowadays, bread still looks fresh after six months, but let's not get into that topic now.

So, I cut off the green parts, rinsed the bread under water for a few seconds, put it in the oven, and after a few minutes, I had warm, almost fresh bread. I ate it with fresh cauliflower straight from the field, sprinkled with salt and dipped in butter.

It was hard work, but I knew it wouldn't be a vacation. I saved every Norwegian crown for my future. Remember this statement, as I'll return to it from a different perspective later in my story.

The day came for me to leave, the end of grueling work on the farm for a waiter from the best hotel in city, where there was plenty of food, warmth, and comfort, even if freedom was lacking. Now, there was no food or warmth, but I had freedom.

I decided to go to Denmark, to Copenhagen, and find a refugee camp to apply for asylum. At the time, Sweden gave me some sort of unusual spiritual allergy. I don't know what it was, but you'll surely discover it yourselves soon.

It was autumn 1987, and the weather was typical for fall, drizzling, sometimes cold, sometimes sunny, and I had to find a place to register at a refugee camp.

I found a police station and decided to ask them what to do next. Suddenly, while sitting on a bench at the police station, waiting for my turn to talk to somebody about my situation, I saw how they brutally treated a man, and witnessing this made my stomach turn with nervousness, forcing me to run outside and vomit.

A storm of thoughts raged in my head, and I began drowning in my own chaotic reasoning. In summary, I had reached a wall in my life, one that I couldn't pass through.

I, who used to run barefoot in the snow at night, looking for dogs to kill if they attacked me, who broke boards and tiles with my bare hands, now doubted myself, and the time of doubt had come for me. The future began to paint my life in the colors of depression.

I left the police station and stood on a bridge, where the water beneath it seemed like a solution to my life's problems. I started contemplating taking an extra step, to fall into that dark, green abyss and end my dilemma. After a while, I realized that I swam too well, and it wouldn't be easy to drown in that canal. I started thinking I needed a quicker method to end it all.

Suddenly, out of the corner of my eye, I noticed two shady-looking guys. With my bags in tow, I decided to lose them in the maze of narrow streets in Copenhagen. On one hand, I didn't know what to expect from them, and on the other, I didn't want to end up in trouble with the police by getting into a fight with some thugs in a foreign city.

I wanted to die without sensation, peacefully, not to disturb anybody. I went to the train station, stored my luggage in a locker, and went out again, searching for a solution.

I met some guys who, for thousands of crowns, guaranteed smuggling me to France.

But I didn't have that kind of money, so I started looking at displays of white weapons in shop windows. Knives with compasses, maps, and flashlights, and an idea started to blossom that I could make my way to France since I spoke the language well, and I would leave Poland as far behind as possible.

Depression, exhaustion, stomach pain, and repeated vomiting, suppressed by smoking cigarettes, made me realize I was wasting my time. I decided to head to the highway and throw myself under a truck. That would certainly be a quick and sure death. I walked on the left side of the highway, choosing the right tool for committing suicide. Now, pay attention because I'm going to talk about the things that saved my life, allowing you, my dear grandchildren, to be here today, listening, reading, or hearing this story.

This isn't a fairy tale, nor is it a made-up story. This is my account of the facts as they happened.

Suddenly, I heard a voice. I can't describe it to you, whether it was in my head or outside of it. A sentence that changed my life:

"You are loved and you are needed. Don't do this, because you will not only destroy yourself but also ruin the lives of others, as the truck driver is likely to have a family."

I turned around, not believing that someone was talking to me, standing alone on the highway. There was no one near me. Shocked by this event, I returned to the train station.

I was now homeless, living at the train station. Well, my plans had failed. Instead of a refugee camp, now I was hearing voices, a complete breakdown, I thought I was losing my mind. Walking around the station, watching people, smoking cigarettes, vomiting occasionally in the restroom, it was a time of utter despair. I was afraid to sleep at night, so I tried to sleep during the day when normal people were moving around from platform to platform, and there weren't too many homeless people, who didn't seem friendly.

At night the Train Station looked like a jungle of crazy, dangerous beings who were trying to just survive the night. At 3:00 in the morning, they closed the entrance to the train station because they were doing a thorough cleaning of the floors. Forced to leave, I stepped outside under the full moon, with my pride as an atheist shattered.

I always tried to convince my friends that God is for those who are poor, ugly, sick, or old. That's what my father used to say, and for a long time I repeated those beliefs myself. But from the depths of my heart, not from my mind but from the very core of my soul, I uttered the most dangerous sentence in the world.

I must emphasize, it wasn't a prayer, it wasn't the rosary, it was a sentence that barely wanted to come out of my throat:

"Jesus, if you really exist, please help me."

You see, I don't care who you are today, whether you believe me or not, though you should. And if you're not part of my family, your opinion won't affect me at all. This is what happened in my life.

A few minutes after I said those words, suddenly, at 3:00 in the morning, a man around my age appeared, walking through the street. He came up to me and, in English, asked me:

"What are you doing here?"

After many years, I have concluded that this simple question is both very profound and complicated, almost philosophical. My answer was simple:

"I don't know and I don't speak English."

As I tell you this story, my dears, I want you to remember that no matter how lost or hopeless you may feel, there is always something waiting for you on the other side of your struggles.

Sometimes, it takes a moment of despair to hear the voice that reminds you of your worth and purpose. And when you do, hold onto it, because it may just change your life.

That mysterious man who appeared before me was from Jordan, a member of the PLO (Palestinian Liberation Organization) in 1987. A Muslim, who stood in front of the Copenhagen train station at 3 in the morning.

In some strange way, we agreed that I spoke better French than English. And miraculously, another man appeared next to us, who was Algerian and spoke both English and French. From that encounter, I learned that he was a male prostitute, selling his services on the streets of Copenhagen.

Well, dear children, as you can see, different people can be put on your path of life, and if you don't have a moral backbone, you might end up in places where no one will admire you.

After several minutes, we agreed it would be a good idea to find a cafe to sit down in and continue our international conversation. It was already almost 4 a.m., and nearly everything was closed, but we found a place where we could get coffee. I pulled out my Polish-English dictionary and tried to string together a sentence in English.

At some point, two young women approached us and began speaking to my two companions. When I saw small plastic bags in their hands, I realized they wanted to sell us drugs.

Now, let's have a moment of honesty, with you and everyone else reading this book.

Other than smoking cigarettes, the strongest thing I ever smoked was Camel cigarettes without a filter, or Sport – Polish cigarettes without a filter. Thank goodness you don't know what those are, only the old guard will know, but they were quite potent. I smoked my first Camel when I was 12 years old, under a wall in the school park, and when I inhaled, I couldn't get up, I was so dizzy.

But coming back to our situation, seeing the drugs, I thanked everyone and said I had to go because I had a meeting in the morning.

Of course, I was lying through my teeth, I was homeless, a lost man whose world had collapsed. But because I think I knew what was right and wrong, I decided to leave them behind.

I went back to my new home. *"Grandpa, do you have a new home in Copenhagen?"* you might ask. Slowly, my dear ones. My new home was the train station. It was just a metaphor, a joke in the midst of my tragedy.

It was already nearly 6 a.m., and I hardly slept. Exhausted from walking, tired of talking with strangers in a language that wasn't mine, I sat down on a wooden bench at the main platform of the station and fell asleep sitting up.

After some time, I don't remember how long it lasted, I felt like my mind was completely blank. Nothing. My brain had fallen out, I couldn't think of anything. Complete emptiness. Suddenly, like a bolt of lightning, I heard a familiar voice.

This time, in English:

"Grab your luggage, get in a taxi, go to the port."

Once again: Luggage, taxi, and port.

I didn't hear anything about where to go, just to the port.

Now you'll see why this must have been a supernatural message. Paying a month's Polish salary for a taxi ride in Copenhagen? I don't think anyone would do that just from hearing a voice. But as you can see, I behaved like a robot, without thinking or questioning what I heard.

When I arrived at the port, I didn't know where the ferries were heading. Seeing a line of people, I simply got in line behind the last person, still not knowing where this line was going.

You must know that in Poland, at that time, standing in lines was so normal that no one was surprised by the number of people lining the street outside a store.

Suddenly, the person standing in front of me turned around, shock! It was the same man who had approached me at 3 a.m.

He asked me another question:

"What are you doing here?"

My answer was almost the same:

"I don't know."

From what I understood in English, he said:

"Whenever I ask you, you never know. Do you want to visit me in Sweden? Do you have time?"

My answer, under my breath was:

"Man, I've got my whole life ahead of me, I have loads of time, and I don't know what to do with it."

But outside, I kept my cool and politely responded,

"Sure, why not?"

You must know that I had a strange aversion to Sweden, I didn't know why, but you'll find out soon.

This Muslim man's name was Stefan. He paid for my ticket, although I insisted on paying myself. Apparently, the amounts weren't large, and we headed to Sweden.

Now my conversation relied heavily on the Polish English dictionary, and I started an accelerated English course with a guy who spoke Arabic, Swedish, and English. None of these languages were my strong suit.

If I can give you any advice, my dears, learn other languages! A wise professor who taught me French once said that there are two types of rich people in the world:

"those who have money and those who know languages."

How true that is; only someone who travels will find that out. And as you can see, I was constantly on the move, on the journey of life, without knowing where I would end up.

* * * * *

Chapter 6

A Strange Country And A Stranger Kindness

The shock of grace, and the first betrayal.

W E ARRIVED IN A SMALL town called Falkenberg, on the east coast of Sweden, between Gothenborg and Malmö.

In Stefan's apartment, there was also an older English man, Mr. Wright. Stefan told me he knew some people who were Christians. They were okay but a little crazy. "Crazy" was the adjective he used to describe them, meaning they were nuts.

I thought to myself, "I'm in trouble," from one bad situation to another. In the evening, we went to a meeting, a service at a Baptist church, a Swedish church in Falkenberg. Remember, Stefan was a Muslim.

But soon, I learned that the reason he knew these people was that, as a man trained in martial arts, he had gotten into a fight and was assigned a probation officer by the court to keep an eye on him.

That probation officer turned out to be an elder in the Baptist congregation.

And, as you can imagine, he gently pressured Stefan to read the Bible. It was like asking the devil to wash himself in holy water.

At the end of the service, someone suggested we all hold hands and pray. I had no choice; I didn't speak Swedish or English, and no one there spoke Polish or any other language I could communicate in. Suddenly, as someone grabbed my left hand and then someone else took my right hand, something happened to me that I had never experienced before. It felt like 220 volts of electricity passed through me. My eyes widened, tears streamed down my cheeks, and I froze. I didn't know what had happened.

I won't comment on what that was just yet, as the time for that will come later. The pastor of this church came up with the idea to give me a Bible. The very same Bible I had criticized my entire atheist life. When he handed it to me, it turned out it was written in Cyrillic, in Ukrainian.

I knew Russian and could read Cyrillic, but it was the Bible, and it's not an easy book to read with just basic language skills. Of course, I kept my composure, thanked him, and we went home after speaking with the people gathered there.

In the following days, Stefan took me to the refugee office, and I started the process of immigrating from Poland. I quickly got a lawyer, based in Malmö, paid for by the Swedish state to handle my case.

I was enrolled in a Swedish language school, and little by little, I began integrating into life in this foreign country, Sweden.

I must tell you that at first, I thought their language was so strange and difficult that I would never learn it. But that was just my initial impression. After a while, I started to distinguish the words and speak as best I could.

Of course, English remained the most popular language, as all the other students in the Swedish language school spoke English, so I was learning two languages at once.

One at home with a dictionary, and the other at the Swedish language school.

Living with Stefan, I didn't know that Muslims were so sensitive about the cleanliness of their food. Somehow, I was missing the Polish cuisine. In my home, my mother cooked amazing food. But here, I was alone, and I missed pork trotters with mustard. You've probably never eaten such delicacies in your life, but in my country, where we didn't have much, pork was very popular, so they used to say:

"*We use everything from the pig except the squeal.*"

I don't know if you understood that, but let's move on. After returning from the store where I bought the pork trotters, I started cooking them with spices, and then finally sat down in the kitchen, eating them, and offering some to Stefan, who looked at me as if I had murdered his mother. It reminded me of the taste that connected me to my Homeland. Pork trotters in jelly with vinegar, or hot with mustard.

I washed all the dishes I had used for cooking, and suddenly I saw Stefan scrubbing the pot I had cooked in, with such force that I thought I had done something wrong. I asked him: "*Wasn't it clean?*"

He responded with such an expression that I realized he was so disgusted by pork that he would have preferred to cleanse the pot with fire, to ensure nothing impure would come into contact with it when he cooked his own food.

I have to admit, after all these decades, I laughed out loud while preparing this story for you.

One evening, I was lying in bed, and suddenly an older man appeared at the door. His name was Yete, and he owned a beautiful restaurant in town.

Stefan introduced him and said he had met him on the street and that Yete might help me find a job. It turned out he allowed me to work in his beautiful restaurant, as a dishwasher.

Yete didn't know that I had been a master waiter in Poland, and besides, my Swedish was so poor that I didn't even bother explaining who I was. My job was to wash plates and pots.

At that time, I thought to myself:

"What have I done?" I had been a master waiter, training my apprentices in the trade, and now here I was, a dishwasher in Sweden, unable to communicate with anyone.

A remarkable career, to put it sarcastically. But, dear ones, let's not despise the days of small beginnings. Remember, to cover a long distance, you must first take a single step.

"When you're in the eye of the storm, the past feels clearer than the future."

Everything collapses around you, and the meaning of the next day seems lost. Today, I can call it faith, believing in something unseen but existing. Or maybe, something that could exist.

School, work, household responsibilities, struggles with understanding a foreign language, people I didn't know would be my new way of life.

Yet Stefan, as if out of nowhere, was always there to help me. He built trust within me, and even invited me to stay at his place, which, as it turned out, wasn't his but belonged to the Baptist Church, which took care of people in need. That's why Mr. Wright was there, a white, elderly man living with a Muslim Palestinian.

Feeling relieved that everything was finally falling into place, I let down my guard. My protective shield was set aside, and I was completely exposed to the approaching catastrophe. Living in constant stress, suspecting everyone of wrongdoing, is not easy.

Life had taught me that not everyone is kind, and among decent people, there's always an iconic Judas Iscariot.

Perhaps the Iscariot clan no longer exists, but their name was forever tarnished by one man, Judas, the one who betrayed Jesus of Nazareth.

"Grandpa, what are you talking about?"

You might ask, does it even matter?

To me, it is very important. This story was like a crossroads, a moment of decision that would change my future and impact your existence. Please listen, be patient.

One day, Stefan, seeing that I was earning money and beginning to prosper, offered me a reasonable solution to my situation, instead of keeping money in the traditional sock, why not open an account and deposit it in a bank? It sounded like a brilliant idea, I thought, unaware of the trap being set for me.

I was working hard *"off the books"* in a restaurant as a dishwasher.

Meanwhile, my proverbial Judas, Stefan from Jordan, was carefully preparing an almost perfect scheme.

We went to the bank to open an account for me, because I couldn't do it; I lacked the necessary documents. Since this man had been so kind to me, why wouldn't I trust him?

I agreed to let him open the account in his name and give me a second card so I could use the funds as needed. It seemed like a great arrangement.

I should mention that in Sweden, at that time, Arabs, called "swart hår" ("black-haired"), didn't receive much sympathy from the Swedes, and finding work was difficult.

Yet here I was, a Pole who had just stepped off a ship, already with a job and making money.

In the heart of my familiar Judas, anger and jealousy began to grow. He waited for the right moment to strike.

Stefan trained in karate, which was something that connected us. We often practiced together in our free time, and I truly enjoyed it. But then came the day of the *"kiss"*, the day of betrayal.

After returning from language school, where I was learning Swedish, Stefan greeted me at the door with my backpack in his hand and a shout that he didn't want to see me in that house anymore.

Shocked by his behavior, I stood frozen for several minutes, outside the building where I had lived for several good months, on the snow, without a penny to my name. My life started falling apart once again. And yet, I thought I had finally gotten back on track.

What could I do? Where could I go? Who could I complain to about the money that had been stolen from me, the money I had earned through hard work, washing dishes in a restaurant?

Over the past few weeks, I had met two Poles living in a refugee camp in Falkenberg. I decided to go to them, as I knew no one else well enough to ask for help of such magnitude. The snow crunched beneath my shoes, which weren't suited for such harsh weather. As I walked, I began to speak from my heart:

"God, help me."

As I uttered those simple words, yet at the same time magical, like the legendary spell *"Open Sesame"* a film unfolded before my eyes... A film produced by Heaven itself. *"Grandpa, what are you talking about?"* you might ask.

Standing on that sidewalk for what seemed like just a few minutes, I watched a film directed by an angelic filmmaker. From the moment I spoke those words at the Copenhagen train station:

"Jesus, if you truly exist, please help me."

I saw how blind and ungrateful I had been. I hadn't realized how God had reached out to me in my time of tragedy.

I hadn't seen how He sent someone to take me to Sweden, a place I had initially rejected.

I hadn't noticed how, the very next day, He brought me to people who follow Jesus. I hadn't understood how I had slowly started taking steps toward legalizing my life in Sweden.

I wept bitterly on that sidewalk, realizing how I had failed to see God's hand in all of these events. I recognized myself as a blind ingrate. With tears in my eyes, I entered the room of my fellow countrymen, with whom I shared this news.

Epithets flew, ones I will not repeat, you can only imagine how my friends reacted to Stefan's behavior.

That day, I was supposed to go to work, so I decided to call my boss and tell him what had happened.

During our phone conversation, I found out that Stefan had gone to the police and told them that I was working illegally in a restaurant and that he wanted nothing to do with me.

Of course, he did not mention to anyone that he had taken my $1,500 and closed the account. My card was now useful only for scraping ice off the windshield of a car, except that I didn't own one.

It turned out that the policeman had called my boss and informed him about Stefan's message. In the midst of this tragedy, another twist emerged, Yete's son had gone to school with this policeman when they were young, and they knew each other quite well.

Yete assured me that a place would be prepared for me at work once I obtained my permanent residency in Sweden.

He immediately called another acquaintance who worked with refugees, and that same evening I ended up in a small hotel. I was assigned a room until my immigration case was resolved.

During my stay in that small hotel, I started training.

On one hand, I felt gratitude toward God for the help He had given me, yet on the other, I saw Stefan, the man who had robbed me of all my hard-earned money in Norway and Sweden.

I had lost absolutely everything. I didn't have a single penny left.

Well, if someone deceives and robs you, it's not easy to accept; you feel you must do something about it. Friends, I wouldn't wish this situation on anyone.

After months of hard work, someone had gained my trust and, without much effort, took everything from me. Today, when I think back on it, that amount of money doesn't seem so big, but at the time, it was absolutely everything I had.

I can say that I was utterly ruined. I started training, preparing my body for a fight of my life.

I couldn't go to work because the police knew about the restaurant, and the owner didn't want to create circumstances for new problems. So, I ran, did push-ups, practiced strikes, meditated, and did everything to regain control over myself and my fate.

Stefan, a man whom God used. I must mention that Stefan came from Umeå, more than 1,100 kilometers from Falkenberg, where he lived. It turned out that he had married a Swedish woman, but after a few years, they divorced each other.

He was traveling by train from her place to his "new" kind of home, a residence belonging to the Swedish Baptist Church. And suddenly, something told him to travel a bit farther, to Copenhagen. He didn't know anyone in Copenhagen. He had no business there.

Yet, under the influence of some strange, unnatural feeling, he decided to go to Copenhagen anyway. After hours of aimless wandering around the city, he ended up at the train station, where he met me. You already know the rest of this story.

I don't know how best to describe it, but I believe that someone watches over our steps. Even though we have free will, people appear on our life's path, people whom God places before us.

They are His vessels, and they don't even know about it. I won't dwell on this topic, but let me ask you something:

Can clay complain to the potter about what he does? Does it even matter? The potter will do whatever he wants, and the clay, and all other tools, can be furious, but they can't change a thing.

The potter is the master, the Creator. Of course, that was just a small digression.

* * * * *

Chapter 7

Opening The Door To Christmas

From rage to recognition, and a knock at the door.

I WAS STILL SITTING IN the small hotel room, watching TV in a language I didn't understand. Occasionally, English-language movies would appear, with Swedish subtitles. I started watching Danish television to get used to the language. But I couldn't focus, anger was eating me alive. One punch to destroy this man. Not a drawn-out fight like in the movies, but one precise blow to take down my opponent.

I know it sounds horrible, but it was a time in my life I did not know anything better than revenge and destruction of my enemy.

It's December 1987, the days are short and cold. Sometimes it snows. Other times, it rains. The weather is so gloomy that I don't even want to step outside. You could go mad with boredom. Suddenly, there was a knocking at my hotel door.

A young couple appeared, asking if I had any plans for Christmas Eve. Of course, I joked that I had an important business meeting and didn't have time for such trivial things.

But of course, I was kidding. I was already so tired of sitting alone in my hotel room, without anyone to talk to, that I gladly accepted their invitation. I had no idea what had happened in the meantime in that small Swedish Baptist Church in Falkenberg.

You must know what was happening outside my hotel room, events that had a massive impact on my life.

[I won't say right now that it affects you too, but if it hadn't happened, perhaps you wouldn't even exist.]

It turned out that these *"crazy"* Christians as Stefan called them were so fervent in their faith that suddenly, things began to happen that were not acceptable to the Baptist Church leaders.

These simple believers noticed, in the pages of the New Testament, that everyone who believed in Jesus displayed certain signs. I won't go too deep into this topic, but I will mention one thing, it was about the baptism in the Holy Spirit. These *"madmen"* according to Stefan, my Judas Iscariot, cried out to God, desperate to experience His power and the Holy Spirit came upon them.

Things began to happen that the Baptists couldn't accept, so a group of about 30–40 people was asked to leave the Baptist Church and continue their faith journey elsewhere.

Luckily, one family had a very large house, so they began holding meetings there, just as had been done in the first century, during the times of the people who walked with Jesus. You might say:

"Grandpa, why don't you say, 'in the times of the apostles'?"

I have a reason. I say:

"in the times of the people who walked with Jesus"

because religion has placed these simple people on such a pedestal that today, when we hear the word *"apostle,"* we no longer consider its true meaning.

We automatically imagine holy people floating 30 cm above the ground and thinking about which prayer to say to them.

We don't realize that the word *"apostle"* means *"sent one,"* a messenger with a message, a person representing the one who sent them. Our religious lenses deceive us. But that's another topic for another time.

Now, these "*renegades*," the overzealous Baptists, facing Christmas holiday to spend it among themselves, were surrounded by people who believe as they do.

However, there is something shocking in the New Testament. Jesus said that He would build His Church, and that those who believe in Him must go into all the world and proclaim the good news to everyone who has breath in their lungs. *"What are you talking about, Grandpa?"* you might ask.

Jesus said they must go to everyone and deliver this message:

> "For God so loved the world, that he gave his one and only Son, that whoever believes in him should not perish, but have eternal life." (WEB, John 3:16)

I won't go into this topic in detail, but these fervent believers began to think intensely.

Who else could they reach? Who else might hear the Good News? They recalled that a few months ago, Stefan had come with me, and they had given me a Ukrainian Bible.

Step by step, they learned that I was staying in a hotel, near their meeting place. So, they decided to send a young couple with a mission to invite me to a Christmas Eve dinner for lonely people. What a brilliant idea!

If you read my book and if you are from this Baptist Church in Falkenberg, please continue this idea, because you will know in a second what had happened to this stranger from Poland.

And at that time, I was very lonely. Abandoned. Forgotten. Rejected. Cheated. Disappointed. Ready for committing a horrible thing to Stefan.

The moment of the visit arrived. It is never easy to enter a place where you don't know anyone, but someone was watching over me! Upon entering the gathering, a Polish woman, about 35 maybe 40 years old, approached me. She had married a Swede. After a few sentences, she shared a secret that would change my life.

Almost whispering in my ear, she told me that the pastor had Polish Bibles and that if I asked him, he would surely give me one for free. Well, I had never held a Polish Bible in my hands before.

Catholic Catechism, perhaps some Gospel passages, prayers to the Blessed Virgin Mary, and other prayer books, YES! I had seen them as a child, under the influence of my beloved grandmother. But an entire Bible?

I had only heard of it. I knew that Jehovah's Witnesses in Poland had it, but among Catholics, it was not common.

Never, let me say that again, never had I seen my grandmother, my mother, my father, my uncle Stefan, or anyone else reading that book or having it on their shelf.

Of course, I gathered my courage and asked the man they called Pastor Lars to give me that special book. (Regarding his name, if my memory serves me right was Lars or Jurgen.)

The Polish lady mentioned that it was free, which sounded quite appealing. Back then, I would never spend money on a religious book. Now, pay close attention.

I'm going to share something you must remember for the rest of your life:

If someone ever requests a Bible, as I did, inquire about the cover color and font size, but NEVER reply

by saying you'll think about it. I beg you, never say that you'll consider it or pray about it.

I don't remember much of what happened after that at the gathering. Evidently, it didn't leave such an impression on me that I would recall it.

I am sure it was a wonderful meeting, and there was plenty of food. But for me, a one thing I will always remember is the woman who told me that the pastor had Polish Free Bibles and could give me one. When I asked the pastor for it, he replied:

"I will think about it."

I don't know why he said that. Maybe it was God's plan? Maybe not, probably so.

But on February 18, 1988, Thursday evening, I was invited again to a meeting at their home, because as I mentioned earlier the group, which was now called "Vinträdet" in Swedish, had been asked to leave the Baptist Church building.

It was cold that day. Almost four decades had passed since that moment. And now, as I write this book on my computer, it is the year 2025.

And speaking of computers. Back then, we had typewriters. Computers were not as widespread as they are now. They seemed like something from another world.

Crossing the threshold of that house, after the host invited me inside, I shook the snow off my boots. Then, I heard the words:

"I have something special for you!"

Listen... I was in Sweden, riding a bicycle in freezing weather. The cold pierced me to the bone.

So, in my frozen mind, I thought, maybe they had an old car for me? But when they handed me a book with a black plastic cover, titled "Biblia Tysiąclecia, Kardynał Wyszyński", etc., I felt a little disappointed.

I thought I was getting a better gift. I had no idea that this day would become a pivotal moment in my life. Not for a second did I believe that this seemingly simple book would influence my life so deeply.

> *[Hello! And just so you know, my life is intertwined with yours. Otherwise... you wouldn't be here! Having spent considerable time documenting the events of my life, I hope you are still reading this book, be patient with this old grandpa.]*

All right, let's continue...

I think there were about 25, maybe 30 people at the meeting that day. The kitchen and living room were spacious, so they could accommodate many chairs.

Whenever I had been there before, someone always sat next to me and translated into English, since everything was conducted in Swedish. My Swedish was still in its infancy at the time.

But that evening, no one sat next to me. No one translated what the pastor was saying. But as I often say, Poles always find a way. Knowing several foreign languages, I concluded that the speech was about the Letter to the Corinthians. At that time, I was not familiar with the Bible to immediately know where that letter was, so I started flipping through my new, free Polish Bible, searching in the index for the right page.

To my surprise, I discovered that there were two letters to the Corinthians, not just one. I realized that I had heard chapter eleven, (of course in Swedish) so I began searching for the relevant verses. Remember, I had never held a Polish Bible in my hands before.

Eventually, I found chapter 11. I highly recommend reading it now or later but listen to what happens next.

> "Therefore, whoever eats this bread or drinks the Lord's cup in a manner unworthy of the Lord will be guilty of the body and the blood of the Lord.

But let a man examine himself, and so let him eat of the bread, and drink of the cup. For he who eats and drinks in an unworthy manner eats and drinks judgment to himself, if he doesn't discern the Lord's body. For this cause many among you are weak and sickly, and not a few sleep." (WEB, 1 Corinthians 11:27–30)

When I finished reading verse 30, something supernatural suddenly took hold of me. I don't want to use Christian terminology, because at that time I did not know it. Even today, I try to speak in non-religious language, so that the average person can understand what I'm saying. No Christianese.

My dear friends, I grew up in Poland. I was born in 1961. Back then, everyone was absorbed into the Roman Catholic Church. Nobody questioned it. It was so normal that if someone dared to do anything different, their entire family and friends looked at them like a lunatic.

I'll return to that memorable day in a moment, but in order for you to fully grasp what I experienced, I need to tell you this. When I was in the military, one day my grandmother Wanda came to visit me. She arranged, I don't know with whom, a leave pass for me, so I could go to the city with her.

Since Easter was approaching, she told me that we needed to go to church and confess our sins.

The holidays were coming, so it had to be done. I didn't want to hurt her feelings by explaining that I no longer believed in God, that such things were for old women like her, who were nearing the end of their lives and probably needed to believe in something.

But for the sake of peace, appreciating the fact that she had traveled over 150 kilometers to visit her first grandson, I went to church with her.

Confession lines were forming at the confessionals, after all, it was the pre-holiday season.

Grandma went first, and right after confessing, she marched to the front of the church, knelt, and continued to pray before the altar. My turn. The line was shortening, but instead of stepping into the confessional; I stood next to a massive pillar, waited a few minutes, and then walked toward my grandmother.

I knelt next to her before the altar, waiting for the priest to give us the wafer for Holy Communion.

I stuck out my tongue, swallowed the wafer, and the matter was settled. I didn't know how this aligned with God's Word, but evidently, God used this moment to show me who I really was.

After reading chapter 11 of the First Letter to Corinthians, suddenly, before my eyes, verse 30 appeared like a projected image. I could see it clearly, standing on the pages of the Bible.

And soon after the projection began, a heavenly Director started showing me something I had never experienced before.

I'll reveal the name of the Director later...

I sat on my chair, alone, without a translator. No one next to me, neither to my left nor my right. I was alone, alone with

> *"Someone who knew my entire life, every detail, every decision, every hidden thought and action".*

And now, He was showing it all to me, like a movie. I didn't cry. I wailed, drowning in bitter tears. I saw my sinful, shameful life, in details that no one could have ever seen or known. I saw myself, walking toward the edge of a chasm, below me, a hellish, yellow-red, putrid abyss.

Hell, with an overwhelming vision, deafening noise, and suffocating stench.

For 90 minutes, I couldn't stop crying. The tears never stopped. I didn't understand what was happening. Or rather, I did. A supernatural being revealed to me who I was and where I was headed.

I was embarrassed, not just because I was crying, sobbing uncontrollably, but also because beautiful Swedish girls were sitting around me.

And yet, here I was, a grown man, whimpering like a child, unable to stop. I tried to control myself. I forced myself to stop. But something inside me wouldn't let me.

I regretted everything I had seen in that open vision. I was disgusted with myself. And then I made a decision:

Never again! I will not go back to that life! I want to know the One who knows me, the One who knows me inside and out.

The One before whom I cannot hide.

* * * * *

Chapter 8

The Breaking Of Bread

*A trembling heart, a whisper from Heaven,
and a new beginning.*

THEN, THE MOMENT CAME WHEN they began to distribute bread and wine. The pastor stood by the table, and people approached taking a piece of bread and drinking a sip of wine.

Something I had never seen before in the Roman Catholic Church as a young boy. Now, I am 27 years old. I thought I had seen quite a bit in life...

I don't know what held me back from approaching the table to take the bread and wine. Was it that verse I had seen, the one that seemed to hang in the air? Or was it fear, a fear that suddenly overwhelmed me?

I sat gripping the chair, holding onto it so tightly as if something might tempt me to stand. I was terrified, terrified that if I walked to that table, took a piece of bread, drank a sip of wine like everybody in this house, I would drop dead. The fear of God was so real, so tangible. And then, I heard a voice.

Right now, as I write these words, I am once again overwhelmed with tears. That moment is so alive in my life that I am sobbing again and struggling to hold back loud cries. Then, I heard a gentle voice:

"I invite you to My table."

I don't know what it was, but I know that it was Him, the One who knows me inside and out. The One who knows my faults, my fears, my questions.

I admit this was not my decision. It was not my own will. I was paralyzed by everything happening. And yet, my hands, which had been gripping the chair so tightly, suddenly let go.

Some invisible force moved me forward. I didn't understand what was happening, but I couldn't resist it. I took a broken piece of bread; I drank a sip of dry red wine and I didn't die.

I lived! I sat back down, and then I heard another sentence from the One who knows me best:

"Go to the pastor and thank him for this gift, for this Book."

I didn't hesitate. I immediately stood up. I walked over to the pastor, who was heading toward the kitchen, and I opened my mouth to say: Thank you for this book. For the Bible. But that was all I could manage. I couldn't say anything more besides that one word: *"Thank you."*

I broke down in tears again. I started sobbing once more. I didn't know what was happening to me. I wanted to stop crying. I wanted to be like any normal person who could simply express gratitude in a normal way. But I couldn't. I couldn't hold back the tears.

When Pastor Lars saw what was happening to me, he gestured to several people, and they formed a circle around me. They began to pray for me. They started asking me questions in English.

My English was very basic, but much better than my Swedish. They asked me:

CHAPTER 8 - THE BREAKING OF BREAD

"Have you been born again?"

I looked at them, completely unable to comprehend what they meant. They asked me again:

"Have you given your life to Jesus?"

I answered honestly:

"I don't know what you're talking about."

Communication was difficult.

Then, they laid their hands on me, it means on my head and shoulders, and they began to pray. From what I understood, one of them said:

"After I remove my hands from your eyes, you will see everything differently."

Alright, I understood that. But when I opened my eyes again, the green evergreen trees covered in snow were still green. I realized that these "spells" hadn't worked on me. Surrounded by a group of kind people, they began singing in Swedish. Expressing their love for me, the love of Jesus. They were very warm, very sincere, lovely people. Even though I didn't fully understand what they were saying.

It was time to go home. I stepped outside, into the fresh air, and started walking toward my apartment. And suddenly...

It was as if a two-ton millstone was lifted from my neck. I felt spiritually upright, I felt as if I could fly. Had I gone crazy?

Had I lost my mind? There was no one around me. I was alone. Alone on a snow-covered sidewalk, heading toward my apartment. And then, out of nowhere, words began pouring out of my mouth, words that made no sense to me.

I was babbling like a total madman. But the joy that overwhelmed me was so great that I couldn't comprehend it.

I have no words to describe what happened.

It was something supernatural, something that went beyond the bounds of normal human experience. Something I had never seen or heard before. Tears and smiles were mixed on my face for a long time, until I reached home.

And what happened next? You would probably ask. No, I did not go to sleep. I opened this new book, this Bible. I read it for so long that I had to reach for a magnifying glass. My eyes could no longer handle the tiny letters under the dim light. I flipped through the pages, hungry, hungry to know more about the One who knows me.

I didn't want to sleep. I didn't want to do anything else. I only wanted to discover, to explore, to learn what awaited me next on the pages of the Bible. What happened to Moses? What about Joshua? What about the Promised Land? There had to be more!

Wherever I went, on the street, on the beach, in a store, I spoke about Jesus. On the beach, people I talked to would ask me: *"Where in the USA do you live?"*

I didn't know how this was possible, after all, I had fled Poland and had become a refugee in Sweden.

Yet, miraculously, people understood me. My English was simple, very basic. And yet, they understood every word I said. But honestly, no one needed to tell me what to say. I didn't need instructions to declare the truth that I am a new man! A new creation!

The Lord Jesus forgave all my sins. I am born again; I have the honor and privilege to call myself a child of God.

> "But as many as received him, to them he gave the right to become God's children, to those who believe in his name." (WEB, John 1:12)

Everything old had passed away, everything had become new. My life was like a fresh, pristine marble slab. I burned with love for people. And at the same time, I couldn't understand why they didn't see it.

But going back to that memorable day, February 18th, 1988,

I had no idea that something had happened in my life, something that Jesus spoke about 2000 years ago. In the New Testament, there is a book called The Acts of the Apostles. I had never heard of it before because, as a young man attending church, I only waited for the moment when the boredom would end, and I could go home after Mass.

I had never read the Bible, so I didn't know its contents. And even if the priest spoke about it, his words were lost in monotony, drowned out by my indifference.

Besides, in my family, at church, and everywhere else, no one ever spoke in other tongues, not in strange sounds, not in spiritual speech, not in anything that resembled it. It simply wasn't part of our world.

It wasn't until I started deeply studying the New Testament that I discovered that speaking in other tongues was described in the second chapter of The Acts of the Apostles.

[I'm sharing this story with you, not because I want you to think that grandpa has lost his mind, but so you can discover something incredible that happened to me.]

"Now when the day of Pentecost had come, they were all with one accord in one place. Suddenly there came from the sky a sound like the rushing of a mighty wind, and it filled all the house where they were sitting. Tongues like fire appeared and were distributed to them, and one sat on each of them. They were all filled with the Holy Spirit and began to speak with other languages, as the Spirit gave them the ability to speak."

(WEB, Acts 2:1–4)

You must understand that although I had studied many foreign languages, no one was able to have a fluent conversation with me in those days, nor could anyone persuade me of anything.

I simply lacked the vocabulary to discuss specific topics in English and Swedish. What happened to me was minimal human intervention.

Instead, supernatural things took place, things I couldn't physically grasp or prove to those who doubted.

I must tell you; I had a friend Marek M., in Poland who looked very much like me. We worked together at a hotel in Poznań and looked like brothers.

One day, he wrote to me and announced that he wanted to visit me because he was traveling to see his Swedish girlfriend. I was thrilled because he was the first person who knew me from my homeland. I don't remember the entire meeting in detail, but one moment remains deeply in my memory.

During our conversation, Marek looked at me and asked me a serious question:

> *"I know you; you are the same Jacek I used to go to clubs with, the same Jacek I used to chase girls with... but who is inside you? Because you are no longer the same person I once knew."*

For those who couldn't find tangible proof of my experiences, the words of my old friend were like an accusation, so direct that it could have convinced a judge to issue a verdict.

You might say:

> *"Grandpa, you lost us a little. What judgment are you talking about? What judge and what verdict?*

Dear ones, I want to tell you that I have become a new person, even though I have the same body.

The one inside me is a different Jacek. Everything old has passed away. Now, everything has become new.

It's as if I wanted to tell a blind man what the sky looks like, how beautiful and blue it is.

But if someone was born blind, they simply cannot comprehend what I'm saying. It is the same in this situation.

A wise and learned man, Nicodemus, once went secretly at night to talk to Jesus. Jesus told him that he had to be born again to see the Kingdom of God, but Nicodemus couldn't understand what that meant.

Similarly, anyone who has never experienced this kind of turning point in life might look at me and think,:

"This guy has lost his mind. All he talks about is Jesus."

Dear ones, if a judge had proof of your wrongdoing, if, for example, you were caught speeding in a residential area, and the camera recorded your violation, then based on that evidence, the judge would sentence you to an appropriate penalty.

What I am talking about is the complete transformation of my life, 180 degrees. My old friend, the one with whom I had committed sinful acts, asked me:

"Who is inside this body? Because this is not Jacek I once knew."

For me, that was the proof that my faith in Jesus had truly transformed me.

If I were to stand before a court today, based on the person I've become and the things I do and say, I would be found guilty of being a follower of Jesus of Nazareth. You'd probably say now:

"Ah, now we understand!" So, there is evidence that you have become a new creation, and people who knew you before are baffled, they cannot comprehend what has happened to you.

Exactly, dear ones. If no one sees the fruit of our faith, then who are we? A painted, decayed tree, trying to hide under a thin layer of paint? That is called hypocrisy, which is falsehood and deception.

But as you remember, I spoke to you about the One who knows me inside out. The One before whom nothing can be hidden. The One before whom we stand naked, with no way to escape or conceal ourselves.

Alright, let me tell you what happened next. I hope you are still with me, my dear family and friends and strangers!

Weeks have passed. For days and nights, every spare moment, I devoted myself to reading the Old and New Testament.

In the meantime, my boss made a call to someone who could help with immigration matters.

And in a miraculous way, I was granted a small apartment, on the top floor, the third floor.

Yete helped me get furniture, an old, big television and a fairly large round table. It was a single-room apartment. The joy was immense! I no longer had to spend years in a refugee camp; I could finally live among the Swedes.

I was learning the language and getting to know new people. I started attending Christian meetings regularly, held in home settings.

However, one thing bothered me, the meetings only took place twice a week.

I missed them so much that I would cry at home, eagerly counting down the days and hours until the next gathering. You are probably tempted to say:

> *Grandpa, why do you say you cried? We don't understand, no one hurt you...*

My dear ones, one day you will understand when you have your own children. When an infant is hungry, it cries until its mother or father comes and feeds them.

Similarly, in the spiritual realm, when someone is truly born again, they are hungry for God's Word and the fellowship of believers. One of the pivotal moments was when my new friend lent me a VCR a video cassette recorder.

I know that nowadays such things are no longer used, but back then, VHS tapes were the size of books, with magnetic tape inside where movies were recorded.

I had a television, but I was missing the player, until the day my Norwegian friend told me I could borrow his VCR for a month, since he was going away to visit his parents.

For me, this was amazing news!

That same day, without hesitation, I jumped on my bike and rode to the pastor's house. I don't remember exactly how many kilometers it was, but it was a long ride. When I arrived at his door, his wife opened it.

"The pastor is not here", she said.

I gathered the courage to tell her that I had borrowed a VCR and wanted to watch some Christian recordings. You won't believe this! This wonderful woman looked at me kindly and handed me only five tapes, each 240 minutes long. I packed them into a plastic bag and hurried home as fast as I could. As soon as I arrived, I made myself something to eat, sat at my round table, and started watching.

One tape after another... I remember one of the tapes featured Ulf Ekman, a former pastor of a church in Uppsala. My English and Swedish were improving, so I could understand him better and better.

Hours passed… Well past midnight, around three in the morning, I was watching a recording of Reinhard Bonnke, a German evangelist who preached in Africa. The title of the film was: "Africa Shall Be Saved".

I was captivated by the message And then, suddenly, as if from deep within my old, massive television, I heard a voice:

"How long must I wait with this gift I have for you? Jesus has paid for it with His own blood."

As soon as I heard it, I turned off the television immediately. I panicked; I had started hearing voices. My heart started beating faster. I sat in silence for a moment.

"Did I really hear that voice? Was it just my imagination?"

I had no idea what had just happened. But I knew one thing, I couldn't ignore it. I shut everything down and jumped into bed, positioning myself in such a way that I wouldn't have to look at the television, facing the wall.

I began to pray:

"Lord, I hear voices. I don't know if I'm watching too many videos or reading too much of the Bible, but I don't want it to turn out that I've lost my mind."

I fell asleep. It was still Saturday… or rather, already Sunday, three in the morning. I woke up, looked in the bathroom mirror, and, smiling at myself, said:

"Jacol (Jack), everything is fine. You're normal."

I went about my morning routine. I took a shower and started drying myself with a towel. I threw it over my back, but suddenly, my hands and the towel froze in place, I couldn't move them even a millimeter.

And then, I heard a voice:

"Do not be afraid, it is I speaking to you!"

I was alone in the apartment. Everything was turned off.

No music was playing. And yet, I heard a clear voice telling me not to be afraid. The moment I heard it; my hands became unstuck.

I didn't think about drying myself anymore, I collapsed onto my knees, naked, wet, on a small rug in the middle of the room. I started praying and crying. I cried out:

"Lord, I don't want to lose my mind, but I hear voices! If You are speaking to me, give me a sign, because I don't want to be a madman!"

That was my mistake, asking God for tangible proof of what had just happened. After moving into my new apartment, Yete had given me loudspeakers with a radio. I had mounted them on hooks in two corners of the room to keep them steady. And then, at the very moment that my lips spoke the words:

"God, if it is You, give me a sign!"

The speaker in the left corner suddenly fell to the ground. I froze. I thought that I was going to poo my pants, well, that I was about to embarrass myself.

But I wasn't wearing any clothes, I was completely naked. The fear was tangible. Tears streamed from my wide-open eyes. I had never experienced anything like this before.

And to be honest? I wouldn't want to experience it again. At that moment,

I remembered the sentence I had heard earlier:

"Do not be afraid, it is I speaking to you."

The first words were:

"Do not be afraid."

Exactly. The One who knows me inside out already knew that I would be afraid. That's why He told me not to fear.

I have no idea how long my prayer lasted. I don't know how long I knelt on the floor. But soon after, doubt began to creep in.

"This must be just a coincidence."

The hooks in the wall could wear out over time. I didn't know how, but that's how I rationalized it to myself. I started doubting what had just happened.

During breakfast, I concluded that I had simply watched too many passionate preachers and read too much of the Bible.

But something still didn't sit right. The brief paralysis in the bathroom, and the voice that I thought I had heard. So, I said aloud:

"Lord, if You are truly calling me to serve You, please, give me one more confirmation. I don't want to make mistakes in life and call myself into ministry. I need to be sure that it is You, and not just me."

I set a condition:

"Today, a preacher from the USA is coming to our church. I don't know him, and he doesn't know me. I am new to this church, just an ordinary person. If he tells me that You have called me to serve You, then I will believe."

Well, it reminds me a lot of the story of Doubting Thomas. The meeting was scheduled to start at around 11:00 AM, maybe 10:30.

But after everything I had been through, I couldn't sit at home any longer. I rode my bike to the building where we were supposed to meet. The doors were locked. But I knew there was going to be a service. So, I waited. I stood in front of the doors... and waited. Before long, the pastor arrived. With a look of surprise on his face, he asked:

"What are you doing here? The meeting is still an hour away!"

I replied:

"I know, I didn't want to be late."

What could I do? Tell him about my inner turmoil? That man had other things to worry about. And me?

My life felt like it was collapsing onto my head, I didn't know how to crawl out from under the rubble.

I took a seat in the last row. The room probably had 50, maybe 70 chairs. People started arriving. But that day, I wasn't interested in small talk, meaningless conversations that led nowhere.

I had a serious dilemma in front of me. Was God really speaking to me?

Or was my mind playing tricks on me? Should I even be here? Or should I have ended up in an institution for the mentally ill instead of attending this service?

Usually, when a guest preacher is introduced at a Christian meeting, he starts the same way:

"Greetings from my church... from my pastor... from my wife... etc., etc."

But this time, it was different. Suddenly, that American preacher stood before us, stretched out his hand, and pointed his finger in my direction. And he shouted, not spoke, shouted! With the passion of John the Baptist, he cried out the exact same sentence that I had heard at three in the morning in my house, as if from behind my television screen.

It was like a spear. As if he had taken it in his hand, gained momentum, and hurled it straight into my heart.

When he finished speaking those words, I stood up abruptly, though everyone else remained seated. At that moment, I wasn't thinking about anyone else.

The spear had pierced my heart. I cried out, like a wounded animal that had just been struck by a hunter's arrow beneath its ribs.

My face was drenched in tears. I sobbed loudly, so loudly that my friend, a few years younger than me, a flight student, rushed to me. He wrapped his arms around me and asked:

"*What happened? Are you okay?*"

I couldn't say anything else except: "*Yes.*"

What was I supposed to tell him? That I thought I was losing my mind? That I had been watching Reinhard Bonnke until three in the morning? That I was hearing voices? That I had been paralyzed in front of the mirror? That my speaker fell off its hook precisely when I begged God for a sign? Was I supposed to tell him all that?

I hope my dears, that now you understand why I have to tell you this, what had happened to me, because I know it is shocking!

"And I can't just die without leaving these events unknown to my family and friends and the rest of the world."

I sat down, like a man devastated by terrifying news. I felt drained. I didn't know what to do next. The meeting came to an end. And I don't remember a single word of the sermon that the preacher gave afterward. The only thing I remembered was:

"*The second meeting will be at 6:00 PM.*"

I rode my bike home. I didn't eat. I read the Bible. I prayed. I couldn't find peace. I was broken. Shattered. I felt like an animal trapped in a deep hole. Totally without escape. Waiting for its death. The clock kept ticking. Hour by hour. And finally, the time came to go back to the meeting. I still hadn't eaten.

I prayed for a miracle in my life. I didn't want to lose my mind. I wanted to be certain that God was truly speaking to me.

This time, I sat on the other side of the room. Where there were three chairs. I chose the middle one.

Before the meeting began, I cried out to God in my spirit:

"Lord, show me that it is You speaking to me."

And suddenly... I heard another sentence.

"Open the Bible!"

"But Lord... where?"

"Anywhere. It is My Word."

I froze. Did I really just hear that? Was it just my thoughts? Was this all really happening? My fingers dug into the spine of the Bible... And suddenly, the book opened on its own.

Right before my eyes appeared the verse:

> "For although by this time you should be teachers, you again need to have someone teach you the rudiments of the first principles of the revelations of God. You have come to need milk, and not solid food."
>
> (WEB, Hebrews 5:12)

I thought, maybe this is just a coincidence, that I had opened to a verse about believers growing in their faith and being able to teach others, rather than continuously needing basic lessons. So, I said:

"Lord, I agree. I am already 27 years old, yet I still act like a child."

And then, again, I heard:

"Open the Bible."

I didn't hesitate. Obediently, I opened the book, knowing it was His Word. I would not argue where or why. And once again...

The Bible unfolded in the same page. I quickly read the verse that my finger landed on, following the voice that commanded me to do it.

> "Nobody takes this honor on himself, but he is called by God, just like Aaron was." (WEB, Hebrews 5:4)

When I finished reading, I turned around and asked the person sitting behind me to lend me their Bible for a moment. I needed to know if what I was seeing in my Bible was the same in someone else's.

Yes, I know, I probably sounded like a full-fledged skeptic. But I had to check. I read the verse again in English.

And then... My eyes filled with tears. I didn't know where they came from. I didn't know why.

I thought to myself:

> *"If my father saw me right now, he would say: ' You weakling! Why are you crying? Straighten up! There is no God! Stop reading this nonsense and do something useful with your life!'"*

But I kept sitting there. Waiting. Waiting for the one percent that I still lacked, the final confirmation I needed, to add to the ninety nine percent certainty I already had, that God was calling me into His service.

Dear ones, you are dealing with a grandfather who did not want to make a life-altering mistake. I did not want to embarrass myself before the world. I did not want to be the laughingstock of my family. I did not want my atheist father to look at me and say:

"This boy has lost his mind."

I had to be sure. This wasn't a joke. I had placed my entire life on one scale, with no safety nets. All or nothing. Black or white. Good or evil.

But I still felt like I was holding a balloon filled with ninety nine percent certainty, searching desperately for the missing one percent.

Then, the preacher announced that he would be praying over the congregation. He walked up to those seated, placing his hands on their heads, praying over them and speaking words over them. I saw this as an escape route. A way to erase everything I was feeling.

A way to forget the last twenty-four hours... Releasing my ninety nine percent balloon and freeing myself from the last twenty-four hours. I said, almost arrogantly:

> *"OK, Lord, if this preacher lays his hands on my head and tells me that You have called me to serve You, then I will believe everything, and the matter will be settled."*

But of course, God's ways are not our ways, and His thoughts are not our thoughts. Once again, I was surprised. I heard:

> *"No one will pray over you; you must believe My words."*

So, with zeal, I stretched out my neck, trying to get the preacher's attention. Just so that this man from America would lay his hands on me, just so he would speak words from God, just so I could convince myself that all of this was simply a coincidence. That was only my imagination. That none of this had really happened.

To this day, I wonder why he didn't lay hands on me. Why didn't he pray over me? Maybe God forbade him. Maybe his thoughts got mixed up. Maybe the preacher thought he had already prayed over me.

I don't know. But I wish I knew. Maybe someday, I will find out. When the preacher walked past me and continued praying over others, despair completely consumed me.

I knew that I was fighting with God. I wanted a way out, if it was all just my idea. But at the same time, I feared the unknown. I feared the great uncertainty. What would I do, serving God?

Writing this, I remembered that unforgettable day February 18th, 1988. The day I was baptized with the Holy Spirit and began speaking in tongues. That day, I heard a sentence:

"I am calling you to be My minister."

At first, I didn't know what '*minister*' meant. When I got home and checked in a dictionary, I read:

"Minister, meaning priest."

I said right away:

"God, I will serve You, but I will NOT be a priest! There is NO WAY I will live in celibacy! NO!"

I had no idea that a minister was not just a clergyman, that a minister is someone like the rudder of a ship, directing it on its course. Today, I know that my calling is to be that small rudder, "mini steer", to guide people toward the One who knows me completely and to be a road sign, pointing the way to the ultimate destination.

He is the One:

- Who rose from the dead.

- Whose tomb is empty.

- Who never wrote a single book, yet libraries are overflowing with books about Him.

- Who never wrote a song, yet He is the theme of more songs than all songwriters combined.

- Who never founded a college, yet all the schools together cannot boast of having as many students.

- Who never marshaled an army, yet no leader ever had more volunteers.

- Who never practiced medicine, yet He healed multitudes without charging a fee.

- Whose enemies could not destroy Him, and the grave could not hold Him.

I am a "mini steer" to the One who stands forth upon the highest pinnacle of heavenly glory, proclaimed by God, acknowledged by angels, adored by saints, and feared by devils, as the risen, personal Christ, our Lord and Savior.

My dear family and friends, I hope you already understand who I am talking about.

Devastated by what had just happened, that I had no choice but to surrender to God.

Suddenly, the pastor's wife approached me. She said she had been watching me all Sunday. And then she asked:

"What is going on with you?"

And I thought no one had noticed me, and simply I did not care about anybody that day.

Hesitantly, I began to tell her, step by step, everything that had happened in the last twenty-four hours.

I don't remember exactly what she said in response, but that short conversation with her was the missing one percent.

It closed my doubts. And then, I ran like crazy, to get home. I was hungry, I hadn't eaten all day. I placed a plate of food on my round table. But before I began eating...

I knew there was something I needed to do first. Remember, my dears, I was alone. I lived alone. The apartment was empty, just me and no one else. No one was watching me... Or at least, that's what I thought.

I raised my hands to the sky, to the ceiling. With my eyes closed, sobbing, I said something incredible:

"Lord, today I give You my life into Your hands. I have absolutely nothing except the breath in my lungs. I have no money, no wealth. I have only my life, but I accept everything You have for me."

I don't remember what happened next... But I felt as if I had lost consciousness. As if a light engulfed my entire being in my room. I stood up, tears still in my eyes, sat down at the table, and began to eat.

* * * * *

Chapter 9

Letter Of Faith

The letter that changed everything.

AND AFTER EATING… I TOOK a paper notebook and started writing letters. Letters to everyone who was in my heart. I wrote the entire night. Until morning. Letter after letter. I had no typewriter. I had no computer. I had no copier to make it faster. There were no emails back then, only envelopes and postage stamps. Each letter was addressed to a specific person. It was April 1988.

I need to take a break. Telling all of this and reliving these memories anew is exhausting. But soon, I will tell you the next part of this story. Just a moment ago, I had to take a tissue again because I was overwhelmed with tears, as every time I cannot forget the moment when I accepted God's calling. It has already been 37 years since that memorable day. I must tell you about another event that happened a few days after I was devastated by the vision of my life at that memorable meeting on February 18, 1988.

As I mentioned before, I worked hard on a farm in Norway. I will not repeat myself or complain about how difficult it was.

However, when, at Stefan's suggestion, I placed my money in the bank, and then he kicked me out of the house, called the police, and robbed me of everything I had, I could think of nothing else but how to get back at him.

I wanted to hurt him, bad. It seemed like a natural reaction, a response to the injustice I had suffered.

The money I had saved was something tangible, a security, just like for any other person. I placed my trust in it completely. There were a few hundred dollars, but today, I would call it Mammon. I encourage you to study the concept of Mammon, it is a fascinating subject.

Yet, on the day I was left without my so-called Mammon,

I turned not to money, which gives a false sense of security, but to God Himself.

After many days of tormenting myself with thoughts of revenge, an evening came that changed everything. That was when I heard a gentle voice:

"Forgive him!"

If today you have $100,000 or more in your account, then $1,500 USD may seem like a drop in the ocean. Maybe you would wave your hand and let Stefan go, but I worked very hard for that small amount of money. Giving it up to someone who stole from me in such a malicious way was not easy. However, at that moment I responded positively:

"I forgive him, Lord."

I experienced something I cannot fully describe to you. It was a feeling of freedom. The burden of hatred and the desire for revenge vanished like morning mist. A new beautiful, sunny day had come, without the dark clouds that had been hanging over my head. I never saw him again.

God used Stefan to lead me to His people, who gave me a book holding a treasure worth giving up one's earthly life. Now at least I believe so I finally understand what Jesus said in His parables.

> "Again, the Kingdom of Heaven is like a treasure hidden in the field, which a man found, and hid. In his joy, he goes and sells all that he has and buys that field."
>
> (WEB, Matthew 13:44)

My decision to forgive Stefan cost me everything I had.

You might say:

"Grandpa, but it was only $1,500!"

Yes, my dears, but for someone earning $30 a month, it was over four years of work, given away in a single sentence:

"I forgive him, Lord."

What lesson does this story hold? I would love to hear how you perceive it in your own lives. As John C. Maxwell once said:

> *"A wise person learns from their mistakes. But a genius learns from the mistakes of others."*

Be geniuses. Keep your eyes wide open to what is happening around you. Learn from what you see and hear. But my story doesn't end here, in the following weeks of my new life, extraordinary things happened.

As I mentioned before, I wrote to everyone God placed on my heart. One of my letters ended up on my father's table.

"Well, Grandpa, did our great-grandfather Jan rejoice when he got it?"

I know you are tempted to ask me that. I don't have good news about him. Before long, I received a letter from him, the only letter I had ever received from my father.

It's a shame I no longer have it, but I remember its contents perfectly.

> *"Son, you are mentally weak. Open the window, throw out that black-covered book, and forget about it. It is not good for you; you need to stand on your own feet."*

When I read those words, a great strength arose within me, a force that compelled me to respond at once.

Even though I had no money and was struggling financially, I put 100 Swedish kronor in an envelope and wrote:

> *"Dear Father, I forgive you for the way you treated me when I lived with you. I now beg you, please use this money to buy a Bible and read it. You told me I was mentally weak, but right now, I am stronger than ever. I was almost at the lowest point in my life."*

And I probably included 100 verses to support my excitement for God's Word. I never received another letter from him. But years later, my sister Anna, told me that everyone concluded I had gone insane.

Does a Prophet Have Honor in His Own Land?

Jesus said:

> "A prophet is not without honor except in his own country and in his own house." (WEB, Matthew 13:57)

Jesus was referring to the fact that the people in His hometown of Nazareth did not recognize Him as a prophet, because they had known Him since childhood and couldn't believe He had a divine mission.

My family knew me well, they knew who I was. So, to them, it was shocking to receive letters from me about a subject they only encountered twice a year, when they attended the Catholic church at Christmas or Easter.

I don't remember exactly how it happened, but I met a Swedish girl.

I don't recall her name, but I do know one thing, God placed her on my path. She was interested in me. She invited me to her home to meet her mother. But at that time, I was deeply in love with Jesus. I wasn't concerned with such matters.

Jesus was always on my lips. I am not saying I became blind, no. I still noticed beautiful women, but my heart burned with love for God and the excitement of discovering new biblical truths.

She worked at a car dealership, where she was responsible for refurbishing used cars to perfection, so the dealer could sell them to customers. I didn't know how this connection would unfold, but... you will hear more about it later.

I can't tell you every interesting detail, because my book would have no end. But I will share one particular event, a church trip to a gathering. I can't say exactly where we were going or why, because that wasn't important. What mattered was what happened on the bus. Among the group of Christians traveling together was a young woman, maybe 25 years old, with long eyelashes, a beautiful face, and a two-year-old daughter.

You read this story, and you probably want to tell me this: *"Grandpa, but what if Grandma Wendy hears about this...?"* Grandma Wendy? Well Gigi, knows this story very well. Don't worry, I have nothing to hide.

I was sitting a few rows behind her, watching as she played with her daughter. The bus started moving, and as I gazed out the window, admiring the landscape, I suddenly heard a quiet voice:

"Sit next to Margaret and tell her what has happened in your life."

Immediately, I thought that was a ridiculous idea. Five minutes later, I heard the same sentence again:

"Go and tell her what has happened in your life."

"No, I won't do it!"

I thought. She might think I was trying to flirt with her, and I wasn't interested in that. Besides, she had a child, and I was certain that approaching her and starting a conversation in my broken English wouldn't be proper.

But believe me, after I refused for the second time, I suddenly heard a firm and urgent command:

"You MUST sit next to her and start the conversation."

This was not my idea! Period! I didn't want to do it, but after the third time, under the pressure of the voice I heard, I walked over to her and asked:

"Do you have a moment to talk?"

"Of course," she replied.

At that moment, a burden lifted off my heart. I felt so much lighter and said to her:

*"This wasn't my idea, but a quiet voice told me that
I needed to speak with you."*

What happened next...? Listen... my jaw dropped when, after several minutes of sharing my story, this young woman said:

*"That's very interesting, because this fall, I'm going
to a Bible school in Uppsala."*

I had no idea such a school even existed. But when she saw my deep desire to know God, she offered to help me get an application form for this school, as they had an international course in English.

"This is no ordinary Bible school," she said.

At that moment, it was as if a bright star appeared in the sky, maybe I would be able to learn more about God, study His Word, and walk the path He had set for me.

In other words, the Holy Spirit guided me toward her so that I would hear about this Bible school.

I saw it as God's divine intervention and began to pray, asking Him what to do next. But there was a problem; I didn't have valid documents proving my legal residency.

My Swedish permanent residency case was still waiting for a hearing. Would I be able to get into the school?

Every day, I prayed, but not only that I fell to my knees beside my bed, took out an English Polish dictionary, and prayed while searching for the right words in English. Each day, I copied passages from the Gospels into a notebook, teaching myself how to write and speak in English, a language I had never liked. But I called out to God:

> *"Lord, give me wisdom so that I may learn this language and proclaim Your Word to the world! Let me share with everyone I meet what You have done in my life."*

Each morning, around 6:00 a.m., the mail carrier would climb the stairs, reach each floor, and slip letters through the slot in the door. But this time, the envelope did not fall to the floor, I was waiting for it like a lottery jackpot! The application form from the Bible school had finally arrived.

When the envelope landed in my open hands, I started crying. I walked to my round table, my hands shaking, as I opened the letter and began examining its contents.

I did not want to wait for anyone's help, I took out my dictionary and started filling out the form, section by section, until it was ready to sign. Just as I was about to seal the envelope, I suddenly felt a strong inner voice telling me:

> *"Don't do it yet."*

I had the distinct impression that I needed to add something to this dry, impersonal application form. I started writing a letter.

First in Polish, then I translated it with my English Polish dictionary.

Its quality? Terrible grammar! But it was 1988, and my English skills were... well... very limited. I wrote something like this:

> *"Dear Director, if you are a servant of God, you must accept me into this school, because I must know God better through His Word. If you do not accept me, you are not a servant of God. God has led me to be in this school. Therefore, I ask for a positive response. Do not ask me how I will pay for the school, because doesn't God care for us more than the birds in the sky?"*

> "Therefore, I tell you, don't be anxious for your life, what you will eat, or what you will drink; nor yet for your body, what you will wear. Isn't life more than food, and the body more than clothing? See the birds of the sky, that they don't sow, neither do they reap, nor gather into barns. Your heavenly Father feeds them. Aren't you of much more value than they?" (WEB, Matthew 6:25–26)

I sealed the envelope and then began praying and fasting. I called out to the Lord, asking Him to touch the heart of the person who would open my letter.

Weeks passed, and still, no response. One day, a friend invited me to Uppsala for a men's conference, featuring American preacher Edwin Louis Cole.

You probably think,

> *"How on Earth could you go to the East Coast of Sweden since you don't have any money?"*

That's true, but we had a plan. We each chipped in 100 kronor for gas, we had free lodging at a friend's place, and as for food, well, you've got to eat anyway, right? I couldn't say no!

At the conference, there were over 2,000 men. At the end of one of the sessions, one of the speakers announced that they were offering a free Christian magazine, so anyone who was interested could fill out a short form and turn it in at the reception desk on the way out.

Of course, I jumped at the opportunity and filled it out. It was free and I was not able to spend any money on such a thing. When I handed it in, the receptionist took one look at my name and suddenly said,

"Please wait, I have a letter for you."

I couldn't believe my ears! How was this possible?! I was attending a men's conference in Uppsala. I had never set foot in this city before.

I had never been inside this building before. There were over 2,000 men in attendance, from all over Scandinavia, and yet, this woman told me she had a letter for me?!

It nearly knocked me off my feet. But the next session with Edwin Louis Cole was about to begin, so I quickly made my way toward the main hall, tearing open the sealed envelope as I walked.

The moment I stepped through the right-side entrance, my eyes scanned the letter, and I saw the words:

"You have been accepted into the first year of Bible school, international class."

I couldn't contain my joy; I shouted at the top of my lungs:

"HALLELUJAH!!!"

The entire hall of men, unaware of why I had just shouted, responded with a powerful *'AMEN'*!

I don't know if you will ever fully understand the joy I felt, but I wish it for you with all my heart. I don't remember exactly how I got back to Falkenberg. I'm sure I floated on wings of joy, with a huge smile on my face. That positive response opened the door to the next chapter of my spiritual growth.

I must tell you that taking the first step is one thing, but taking the second step is a completely different story. I would like to share with you how I was healed. Back in Poland, I had stomach problems.

I didn't know exactly what it was, but I tried to treat myself because I was young, and in my mind, a doctor was only needed for broken bones, not for something as "simple" as a stomach issue. I didn't realize that the stomach is an incredibly important organ, often described as the "second brain" in our body.

I probably had hyper-acidity, heartburn, and irritation of the esophageal mucous, so I drank a special liquid, some kind of medicine with a fairly white color. But now, like magic, my symptoms had almost disappeared.

After my baptism in the waters of the Kattegat Strait, which connects the North Sea to the Baltic, I was invited to a barbecue by my friends. Unfortunately, I forgot the name of the host. I hope he forgives me if he is still alive, but I remember he had a beautiful wife and six children.

They played a huge role in my spiritual growth, as I loved spending time with them. A very kind family. You probably would like to ask me about the baptism in water as I didn't mention anything about it?

My dear ones, it happened in cold seawater, after many prayers and months of radical changes in my life. At that time, I had no idea how significant water baptism was. I only began to discover it later. Because that's a topic too important to summarize in one sentence, I will devote more time to it.

During a game with children in their huge yard, next to their big house, a random misfortune occurred; I got injured by a pine branch.

The injury was so severe that a red spot appeared on the white part of my eye. The pain was unbearable; I didn't know what to do. It hurt when my eye was open, and it hurt when it was closed.

I politely apologized to the family and guests and told them I needed to go to the hospital in Falkenberg.

I hopped on my bike and rushed home to grab my necessary documents.

Then I got back on my "two-wheeled chariot" and sped toward the hospital, praying constantly, as the pain was excruciating. When I was about 50 or 75 meters away from the hospital doors, suddenly, I heard the quiet voice of my Lord:

"Why don't you ask me to heal you?"

The hospital doors were opening and closing, automatically, and at that moment, when I heard those words, I stopped my bike. I felt ashamed, very ashamed. I turned around and started riding back home, apologizing to the Lord Jesus for not even thinking to lay hands on myself and pray for healing.

You might think that this is far-fetched! Maybe you've never heard such a story from anybody in your life. I felt as if I had betrayed Jesus by not asking Him for help.

I thought that sin, character growth, and spiritual matters were one thing, but healing?

My own healing? That was a completely different issue. I stood in front of my bathroom mirror, placed my right hand on the area around my eye, and started praying.

"Lord, forgive me for not turning to You for healing. I am truly sorry that I didn't even think of this kind of prayer. Heal the sick, cleanse the lepers, and cast out demons. Freely you received, so freely give."

(WEB, Matthew 10:8)

And I was sick. I needed healing. I could have asked my friends to pray for me, but apparently God wanted to show me something different on my journey of faith. I went to bed, still praying. In the morning, I was afraid to go to the mirror and look at my eye. I was scared to open it, I didn't want to be disappointed.

But when I finally did, I froze. Nothing! No trace of the injury. I started blinking, touching my eyelids, checking if anything hurt. Absolutely nothing! I was healed! My faith began to grow like yeast in bread dough…

Weeks passed, and I faced another mountain to climb. I had to go to Bible school, but I had no money and no way to get there. Each month, I received a small sum of money from the immigration office for food and hygiene products. My housing was covered, so I didn't need to worry about rent.

But how could I afford to move to Uppsala?

* * * * *

Chapter 10

Provision And The Red Volvo

When God provided through unexpected hands.

ONE NIGHT, I HAD A dream; I saw myself in a red Volvo. I felt that this wasn't just a dream. I started praying and told no one about it, but out of curiosity, I started checking car catalogs for Volvo prices. The prices were astronomical. I was broke, but I had a dream, and I trusted God.

So, I prayed for a vehicle that would get me to Uppsala in the fall. I planted my prayers but kept silent. I didn't want my friends to think I had lost my mind praying for a car.

One day, a man from my church approached me and asked:

Would you help me paint a few rooms in my new house?

He told me plainly:

"I know you can't legally work yet, but I'm asking you for a favor."

I liked this man and his family, so I agreed without hesitation. I don't remember how many days I helped him, but this one thing stuck in my memory.

At the end, he invited me for dinner, thanked me for my help, and as I was leaving, he handed me an envelope full of cash.

You have no idea how my prayer materialized! For me, this was a miracle. A few days later, I got a phone call from Yete. He asked me if I could help him. His restaurant was short on staff for a major event, and he urgently needed waiters. He said, "Not for dish-washing, but for serving tables."

> "But what about the police?" I asked,
>
> "Don't worry, this isn't a permanent job. It's an emergency, and I need you!"

And once again, out of nowhere, money flowed into my pocket! My joy was indescribable. Finances started pouring in; doors were opening.

A few days later, my friend, the Swedish girl, who worked at a car dealership and knew a lot about cars, told me:

> "There's an old, dark red Volvo 240 parked outside. The price is quite reasonable."

I hadn't told anyone at church about my dream, but I figured I could share it with her since she wasn't part of the community.

I went to the parking lot, walked inside to talk with the boss, and asked about the price. The dealer gave me a much higher price than I could afford.

I don't know where my bargaining skills suddenly came from, but I said to him:

> "Sir, this car needs a lot of work. There are holes in the doors caused by road salt, and they need fixing. I'm a buyer, but I can only offer this much, not a single coin more."

The dealer insisted on a higher price. I stood up, thanked him, and started walking out. And yes, just as you might have guessed, my bluff worked. The dealer agreed to my price, and we sealed the deal.

CHAPTER 10 - PROVISION AND THE RED VOLVO

I became the owner of Volvo 240. I only knew one thing about the car; it needed some patching up. Luckily, the engine was indestructible.

Weeks passed, and finally, the moment came to set off to the other side of Sweden, Uppsala. Fortunately, it wasn't Winter, just Fall.

I said goodbye to my church friends, locked up my apartment tightly, and set off in my fully packed Volvo toward the eastern coast of Sweden, 550 kilometers from Falkenberg to Uppsala.

I won't tell you everything, because we don't have that much time, but I'll say one thing, my first days at Bible school were worth telling.

You have to understand that in Poland, the first day of school is like a holiday; we always dress up for the occasion, like going to church.

So, keeping with tradition, I dressed elegantly: A silk blazer, a proper shirt, a tie, polished shoes, a perfect hairstyle straight out of a magazine, and under my arm, a leather briefcase, which someone once gifted me.

Upon arriving, I met up with Margaret, who had also made it to Uppsala with her daughter.

As I was standing in a crowd of international students from all over the world, from every continent, from every race, someone approached me and said:

> You look so sharp! We'd love to take a picture of you for the Bible school magazine.

From what I later heard from friends, at first, when people saw me, they stepped aside to let me pass, because they thought I was a lecturer from the USA!

It makes me laugh to think about it now, but looking back, it was almost prophetic, something that would come true decades later.

At the end of the first day, I went to the reception desk, after checking every single announcement pinned on the walls. I found nothing about room rentals for Bible school students.

I asked the receptionist, and she looked at me as if I had just walked out of a fashion catalog. She said:

> *"I'm sorry, but the school doesn't help students find accommodations. If anything comes up, I'll let you know."*

But most importantly, I was at Bible school!

I had experienced new birth, Holy Spirit baptism, water baptism and speaking in tongues. I had been healed from stomach problems and a wounded eye. I had witnessed financial miracles. I had arrived at school in my own Volvo. So, finding a room wouldn't be difficult! I went into town, checked the train station, used the bathroom, and took care of my physical needs.

You might think, why this man is talking about physical needs. I'm sorry, but I must, because this is part of the story. And soon, you'll understand why.

Remember, I once lived at a train station in Copenhagen. Every experience teaches you something.

Evening was approaching, and I needed to find a place to sleep in my car. No matter where I went, nothing seemed right.

Finally, exhausted from an entire day of traveling, I found a well-lit spot. Sitting in the driver's seat, I pulled my blanket up to my chin and fell asleep, completely drained.

Of course, I prayed and thanked God for a roof over my head. I thanked Him for my car, which allowed me to bring everything I needed with me, and naturally, I thanked Him in advance for the room He had prepared for me. Once again, expecting a miracle.

At around 6:00 AM, as the sun began to rise, I opened my eyes. Suddenly, through the foggy windows, I saw... people staring at me. Confused, I had no idea what was going on. Then it hit me, I parked overnight at a BUS STOP!

People waiting for the morning bus were watching the guy wrapped in a blanket, sleeping peacefully in his car.

I must admit, to this day, I cry with laughter when I think about it. Of all places I could have chosen, exhausted from my journey, I parked at a BUS STOP! Well, sometimes foolish things end up being the funniest.

Of course, my first steps were to the train station. For 50 öre (roughly 10 cents), I entered the restroom, and that's where my transformation took place. I took care of number one, number two (if you know what I mean), and then I took a shower in a sink barely the size of my two hands. Naturally, water was everywhere, but I didn't care.

I shaved, splashed on some cologne, paid attention to every detail, the full "nine yards"!

I put on a fresh shirt, and when I walked out, I looked like I had just stepped out of a high-end barbershop, clean, smelling good, and ready to take on the day!

After several hours of classes, I went back to the reception and asked again:

> *"Had anyone left a note about a room for rent for a Bible school student?"*

Nothing. Once again, no answer. So, yet another night under the stars, sleeping in my Volvo.

That was the beginning of my boon-docking adventure in Sweden, what today is known as van-life, a trend among young travelers who live in their vans.

The next morning, train station restroom again, then back to class. From the outside, I probably looked like a guy with money, driving a Volvo, dressed sharply, smelling fresh, clean-cut, always in new clothes.

No one would have suspected that I was homeless. No one knew I was sleeping in my car. Sometimes even... at bus stops!

Another trip to the reception. By now, the lady recognized me in the crowd of students. When I approached her in my silk blazer, she hesitantly said:

> "You probably won't be interested, but there's an older couple who needs someone to help with their Garden, in exchange for a room for a short time."

Wow. When I heard that, it felt like heaven was smiling at me.

> "Of course, I'm interested!" – I replied.

> "But they expect actual garden work" – she added.

And with full confidence, I said:

> "We can do all things through Jesus our Lord! Give me the address please?"

This was a turning point in my prayers. I had been calling out to God for a room with a bathroom, and now, here it was.

When I arrived, I saw a house surrounded by a high hedge. The hedge was so tall that you couldn't see anything over it. I grabbed my Bible, tucked it under my arm, and rang the doorbell.

The door opened, and there stood Margit (meaning "pearl"), an elderly lady who had spent many years as a missionary nurse in Tanzania.

Of course, they wanted to get to know me; after all, I was going to be living under their roof! An interrogation began. Just kidding, it was actually a wonderful conversation.

I was not in a hurry. Well, as you know, I only *"summarized"* my testimony to two hours instead of six!

Satisfied with what they heard, they said:

"Bring your things, we'll be waiting for you."

And I replied:

"But I have everything with me."

All they saw was me, with a Bible tucked under my arm. They didn't know that behind the tall hedge, my Volvo was packed to the roof! For a moment, they stood puzzled, probably thinking...

"Is this young man's only possession his Bible?"

And maybe, in the end, that's the most important thing anyone can have. *God's Word!*

I must tell you about a few situations that had a huge impact on my new life. Let me remind you that the apartment in Falkenberg, paid for by the immigration office, was now empty, and I had no money to pay for housing in the new city.

The funds I had arrived with were dwindling mercilessly. Travel to school, food, fuel, and other expenses, everything was draining my savings.

I helped Margit and her husband in their garden. They were pleased, of course, but I knew it was only a temporary arrangement.

Their daughter was coming back from abroad, which meant that soon I would have to leave their home. I had been aware of that from the very beginning.

I managed to find a room nearby, a separate space in a house with a bathroom and a tiny kitchenette. I had to pay for a month in advance, plus an extra month as a deposit in case of damages.

I was left with almost no money. I was waiting for the next payment from the immigration office, which was supposed to cover my food expenses. And just then, my car battery started failing. There were days when I had serious trouble starting my beloved Volvo.

Last night was tough. I prayed for a miracle because I had no money to pay for my stay in their house. I had spent everything on the new rental and still needed a new battery.

In the morning, during breakfast, I gathered up my courage. I felt I had to ask:

"How much do I owe you for this month?"

The chair beneath me seemed to be burning. I didn't know what my second sentence would be, but I felt I had to say it. Suddenly, I heard:

"We see that you have a problem with your car battery. We want to bless you so you can buy a new one and not worry about your car. And as for the room... You helped us in the garden, and we are very grateful to you."

A whole sleepless night, my prayers reaching the heavens, and then, at breakfast, another financial miracle!

I found a job at a local newspaper, delivering papers to private homes and apartments. Every morning, at three or four o'clock, I picked up hundreds of newspapers.

I had a special notebook, ran from door to door, and climbed to the fourth floor with a stack of newspapers on my left forearm.

My fitness level was excellent. Obesity? I didn't even know what that was back then. It didn't exist in my vocabulary.

I returned home around seven in the morning. I took a shower in my bathroom, which didn't actually have a shower, only a sink. My left forearm was black, not from dirt, but from ink that seeped through the fresh newspapers. I quickly ate something, rushed to my car, and drove to school.

The school doors closed promptly at eight o'clock. If you were even a second late, you had to wait for the next lecture. Show up late three times, and you'd be sent to the principal to explain yourself.

I never had a problem with that. I was late only once during the entire school year. After spending one class sitting in the hallway, I made sure to arrive thirty minutes early every day, rather than one second too late.

The books we had to read, I devoured them three times.

You may ask, *"Were they that interesting?"*

Yes, they were. But back then, your grandfather had to translate every sentence under the original text to make sense of it.

I would fall asleep at my desk in the evenings. Wake up with my head on the table, move to bed for a while, and then, at three o'clock in the morning, I was back picking up newspapers, and starting the day all over again.

School was amazing. I discovered things I had never heard of before, and I had friends on my left and right.

Soon, I'll tell you about a story that stuck with me to this day. But now, let me tell you about how I had to find a second job, because I still didn't have enough money. I came up with the idea of finding work in a restaurant.

Unfortunately, everywhere required fluent Swedish, and by then, I spoke much better English, because I was at a Bible school where classes were taught in English.

I had finished a year of language school in Swedish, but now I spoke English daily. I wandered around the city, searching for a job, and reading ads. One day, passing by a restaurant, I saw a sign:

"Help Wanted Immediately Dish-washing."

I had been a master waiter in Poland. I worked in the best hotel in the city, and now, I'm asking for a job washing dishes! It was a life lesson I had to go through.

We all have some pride, and some dignity. I struggled to go in and ask for that job. Thoughts swirled in my mind: My father would die laughing:

> *"Son, that black book has led you astray. You used to walk like a peacock in your restaurant, and now you're scrubbing dishes in the West. A horse would laugh."*

I was alone. No one stood beside me. Yet, I felt the weight of those words crushing me.

> *"What will people say?"*

In my twisted imagination, I feared making a mistake. I feared being ridiculed. I marched home on foot. I had no money for gas.

The fridge was nearly empty, the cabinets stripped bare. Poverty had big eyes. It stalked me from every corner. I fell to my knees in my room.

> *"God, help me overcome my own pride."*

Prayer. Crying out. Sobs. Restlessness. The cabinets were empty, but my head was full of human pride. Then I realized:

> *I must be broken. My ego must die. I cannot serve God if I am too proud to take an honest job. Not stealing, but working and earning money, where someone truly needs help. I remembered how Jesus took the bread at the Last Supper and began breaking it. Surely, you remember that. I had a revelation.*

> *If bread isn't broken, it's useless. It must be torn into smaller pieces to be eaten. Only then does it become nourishment. Only then is it useful to the body. I understood that I, too, had to be broken. I had to allow God to use me. I had to become useful in His hands.*

Pride was put aside. I went back to the restaurant and asked if they still needed someone for dish-washing.

I told them I was a student at the Bible school, the one the whole town and all of Sweden had heard about.

After a conversation with the owner, we agreed on my working hours. I could start the next day. They were simply overwhelmed with dishes during lunch hours.

By the way, I did not ask how much they would pay me. I know it sounds crazy nowadays, but whatever they would pay me would help me to have food in my fridge. They needed urgent help.

The next day, after school, I parked my car and ran to the restaurant. There were so many plates and dishes that I couldn't even be seen behind them. I prayed quietly in tongues; it was normal for me. I wondered how to tell them about Jesus.

After all, I was a Bible school student. I felt obligated to share the Good News with them. Suddenly, amid the clatter of plates, glass, and pots, I heard a soft voice:

"Don't say anything. Not a single word."

I stopped. My grandmother would have said that it was the devil sitting on my shoulder, pulling me away from my calling. He didn't want me to talk about Jesus.

My natural instinct was to rebuke that thought. Then I remembered the words from the Bible:

> We reject proud ideas and arguments that go against knowing God. Instead, we take control of every thought and make it obey Christ. And we're ready to confront any disobedience, once your own obedience is complete.
> (Paraphrase of WEB, 2 Corinthians 10:5–6)

I didn't know what to do with this feeling, but again, I heard that I was not to preach to anyone, so I focused on washing dishes.

Every day: waking up at 3 a.m., picking up hundreds of newspapers, then school, then working at the restaurant, then grocery shopping mainly for products with red labels, meaning they had almost expired. Weeks...months flew by!

I had a burning desire to preach to people, but I was caught up in work, and in the evenings, I fell asleep over my required schoolbooks. I can't remember exactly when it happened, maybe before I got the job at the restaurant.

The cupboards were empty. I was driving on fumes, but that Thursday, I decided to go to an evening service at church. The same place where the Bible school was. I had 20 kronor left.

No more money. Nobody would have guessed I was smiling and happy, even though I didn't have a penny left in my pocket.

I walked into the church hallway and went to the cafe. I saw Joseph from Ghana, who now lived in Norway. I asked:

"Would you like to have coffee with me?"

He agreed, we talked, though I don't remember what about. Afterward, I went to the main hall for the service.

During the offering, I threw in my last 10 kronor, but this was not an ordinary offering. I prayed:

> *"Lord, I just had my last coffee with Joseph. The cupboards at home are completely empty.*
>
> *The fridge has ribs, but only the metal ones. My gas tank is empty. I don't know what to do next. Please, help me."*

I knelt and prayed quietly. Nobody heard my cry.

During worship, I lifted my hands, praised, and thanked God for what He had done for me and for what He was still going to do. The service came to an end. I was about to turn and leave when suddenly, a middle-aged couple turned around and handed me a banknote.

> "The Holy Spirit told us to give this money to the person sitting behind us."

OK! If anyone ever tells me that God doesn't exist, that He doesn't hear our prayers, I will burst out laughing!

I am not sorry for what I am going to write now:

> "such a person who thinks that God doesn't exist is a fool, stupid, arrogant, moron! I can write that, as I was such a person, a total idiot."

I had given 10 kronor, and an hour later, I received 1,000 kronor. 99 times more. Nine thousand nine hundred percent. That is what you call a financial miracle. I had no idea this would happen. It was not planned. It was not calculated. It was a miracle.

I went shopping and filled up my car with gas. I invited other students who were also struggling financially for dinner.

One night, as I lay in bed, I spoke to God:

> "Lord, when I see some people preaching, I feel like I could do it so much better! I have this deep desire to speak to people, but now, all I do is work and study."

Then, I heard a soft voice:

> "Get up and go to the bathroom."

Confused, I got up like a robot. I stood in front of the mirror in my tiny bathroom. Then I heard:

> "Speak. Convince him about what you believe in."

I said:

> "Lord, but that's just me! There's no one else here."
> I began to speak, but within five minutes, my topic ran out.

I went back to bed disappointed. My sermon to myself lasted only five minutes. The next night, I woke up covered in sweat.

I had a dream or was it a vision? It was so clear! I was on a massive ship. On board were wealthy Americans, but the flag on it was Norwegian.

The ship was being tossed by enormous waves. Towering waves. People were terrified.

They cried out for help. I stretched out my right hand to save them. I shouted: *"Jesus will save you!"* The image was so powerful, so vivid that I wrote it all down in my notebook.

Meanwhile, school and work continued at full speed. Now, let me tell you about a situation that ended up on the lips of the Bible school director himself. It involved me and my friends. You might say:

> *"Grandpa, you must have been a model student, if the director of such a big school mentioned your name!"*

Hmm! Listen to my story first.

My friend from school, a student from Singapore, was living with a family expecting a baby. One day, he called me and our group of international classmates.

Something terrible had happened. When we met up he told us that the woman renting him a room had received devastating news from her doctors. Her 5-month-old fetus was dead.

They had to operate immediately. Shock. Silence. But us? People of faith. Students at the Bible school. Those who studied the Word of God every day.

We had learned that Jesus commanded us to:

> "Go into all the world and preach the Good News to the whole creation. They will lay hands on the sick, and they will recover." (WEB, Mark 16:15–18)

and also:

> "Heal the sick, raise the dead, cleanse those who have leprosy, and cast out demons. Freely you received, so freely give." (WEB, Matthew 10:8)

We couldn't just stand by and do nothing!

The five of us jumped into my Volvo and rushed to the hospital.

In the parking lot, we began to pray. If someone had stood nearby, they probably thought we were killing someone in my car. We prayed as if our own lives were on the line. The prayer was intense. Loud. Authoritative. Full of faith.

The windows were completely fogged up, five people fighting against death itself. We had to raise that unborn child back to life.

We entered her hospital room. She was lying there, sharing the space with three other patients. We surrounded her. We held hands. We rebuked death itself. The death of her child. The child that doctors had already declared dead.

After a few minutes, a doctor entered the room. Two nurses followed him.

"Wait a moment. We'll move her to a private room. There, you can pray."

We waited. Once she was wheeled into a separate room, we continued to fight for her child. Loudly. Unyielding. Our prayer was our only weapon.

And then? The next day... In the main auditorium. 1,500 students from all different years. The Bible school director, Ulf Ekman, walked to the center.

I only remember one sentence:

"From this day forward, you are forbidden from entering any hospital to raise the dead."

And so, our mission to resurrect the dead came to an end. He told everyone that a group of students had attempted to raise a dead fetus the day before.

But that wasn't the end of our work. Another time, we planned to go to a student dormitory in Uppsala to preach the Gospel to students from other universities.

Again, we sat in my Volvo, praying for God's guidance. It was a time when we could practice our faith in a place that, you could say, was like Sodom and Gomorrah.

We waited for someone to open the door to the dormitory.

That way, we wouldn't have to explain over the intercom that we wanted to talk about God. We entered one of the floors. We saw that the door to the communal kitchen was open. Inside, students were cooking their meals...

And then, another extraordinary story began.

In the corner stood a table with several chairs. We were in the dormitory, among young students. No one looked at us suspiciously, even though we didn't belong in their building.

We started conversations with various people as they entered the kitchen. We were looking for someone open to what we had to say. After a few attempts... After mocking remarks thrown at us by the people cooking, suddenly, a young man, probably from China was asked if he would like to talk about God.

He answered: "I've never heard things like this before. I'm very interested." Wow! For us, it was a gift straight from heaven.

We shared the Gospel with him for about an hour. Then we prayed for him. We arranged to meet in the Bible school building.

Days later, we met him already transformed. Baptized in water. With a heart burning for the Lord. I don't know who was happier, him or us. We had witnessed a seed planted, sprouting and bearing fruit.

This is just one of many stories I wanted to share with you. But I must tell you one more...

One day, I received an official letter from the immigration office. My application had been rejected. I could appeal, but I had no chance of getting permanent residency in Sweden.

It felt like a bolt of lightning from the clear sky. I was crushed by the news.

I still had a few months left to finish school, but suddenly everything had been cut short. There was nothing left to do but pray for a miracle.

At school, they said that if someone needed prayer, they could go to a group of people who would pray with them. So, I went to them. I told them my story. We stormed heaven with our prayers. I also had to share the news with my closest friends from class. Everyone could see that I was deeply troubled.

I had no idea what to do next. What was supposed to be my next step? I felt like an animal trapped in a cage. No way out.

In my class, there was Wilma a short, young Filipino woman, about my age, not yet thirty. Humble, quiet, patient. Like ointment on a wound. When I told her about my situation, she quietly said:

"I will pray for you."

When a person doesn't know what to do next, it's best to call on God for help, rather than seeking escape in alcohol or drugs. After a couple of weeks, Wilma approached me.

"I have good news for you."

I looked at her in disbelief.

"Your case has been heard. It is settled."

I didn't expect her to say something so unbelievable.

Remember, I was in a school where people were completely dedicated to the Lord.

Some would float 30 centimeters above the ground. They were so spiritually intense that sometimes, it was better to stay silent. Forgive my sarcasm, my skepticism, but back then, I was a very young Christian.

When others said:

"I have been in the Lord for 10 years."

"I have been in the Lord for 15 years."

I would say:

"I have been in the Lord for 12 months."

One year sounded weak. But 12 months? That had a stronger impact.

Wilma, if you are reading my book, forgive me, sister. I was young. I was inexperienced in faith. I had difficulty focusing on other important matters in my life because the threat of deportation was hanging over me.

The only thing that brought me joy was knowing that I was now a servant of God and studying at a school to become more effective and to better understand what had happened in my life.

On the other hand, I wanted to complete my studies because I had no idea what the future held, in a week, a month… I had no clue.

Suddenly, I received a summons to the Dean of the Bible School. There were only a few months left until graduation, and now, unexpectedly, I had a meeting with the Dean.

The matter was clear; this was the first time I had been called regarding my outstanding school fees.

Clearly, my Bible verses about God caring for us more than the birds in the sky were not enough. Institutions like these need money to function.

I completely understood them, but I couldn't fathom how my situation could be resolved, as my finances barely covered basic necessities.

The Dean asked me to return my student ID, which allowed me to enter the school building. Of course, I would get it back once I settled my outstanding payments.

As if that wasn't enough, I received a summons from my lawyer in Malmö. At the time, I lived in Uppsala, so I had a long journey ahead to meet him.

I had never met him before. He was a court-appointed lawyer handling immigration cases.

I knew I had to attend this meeting. I locked the time in my mind; I was supposed to be there at noon, exactly 12 o'clock that day.

(Today, nearly four decades later, I don't remember the exact date, but the time is embedded in my memory bank.)

Back then, I didn't have a credit card. If you had money, you could buy things. If you didn't, you had nothing. Nowadays, you might not have money, but you always have a card, so you can get what you need and become a slave to banks that "generously" hand out plastic while charging you 30% interest per year.

God, thank You that I didn't have a credit card back then. I had to believe and wait patiently for miracles instead of solving my problems with credit card without even turning to You.

With my last money, I bought a train ticket to Falkenberg. I couldn't afford to drive my car such a long distance.

There, I met my first pastor. Lars... or maybe Jörgen?

(Forgive me if you're reading this. I don't remember your name exactly, but I remember your face.)

He welcomed me into his home with joy, asking how I was doing in Uppsala and at school. This was not a time for enthusiasm.

121

I had received a rejection from the immigration office, a summons to meet my lawyer, and now I had no access to my Bible school until I paid my overdue fees.

He looked at me, and I believed something in his heart told him that he needed to help me.

He pulled out a checkbook, wrote a check to cover my debt at the Bible school, and added something extra. He said:

"Brother, we are praying for you and believe that God will make a way for you."

He probably saw me as a young man who had fled a communist country, had found God, and was struggling to survive in Sweden.

I thanked God and this pastor for his kindness. To this day, I am eternally grateful to him and his family, truly wonderful people of God.

I continued my journey to Malmö to meet my lawyer. I had prayed about this meeting at noon, not knowing what awaited me afterward. I arrived in Malmö a few hours early. There were still two hours left until noon. I walked closer to the office where my lawyer worked, nervously checking my watch.

Finally, the clock approached noon, and I arrived ten minutes early so I wouldn't be late. Suddenly, a sixty-year-old Polish woman stood in the doorway and started shouting at me. I froze, not knowing what was going on.

"Why are you an hour late?

I am your translator, and I don't have time for this meeting because I have another appointment elsewhere!"

I couldn't believe this was happening. I was always punctual, I hated being late, and I always made sure to be on time. And yet, my fellow countrywoman tore into me...

What a shame. I had traveled 650 kilometers across Sweden. I had walked in front of the building for almost two hours so I wouldn't be late.

Yet, somehow, this mistake happened. I couldn't understand how.

The lawyer looked at me, standing there with a worried face, completely defeated by this timing mistake. I began apologizing to him in English, explaining that I was convinced I was supposed to be there at 12:00, not 11:00.

Suddenly, this very large man, probably three times my size, asked me a question, clearly surprised, while my angry translator stood by:

"Wait, you speak English?"

I replied:

"Yes Sir, I have been living in Uppsala for several months, and I am a student at the Bible school."

When my translator heard that I was studying at a Bible school, it was like something erupted inside her. With nervous movements, she declared that she couldn't translate for me and had to leave immediately.

The lawyer then asked me:

"Will you be able to answer my questions in English?"

"Of course!" I replied, and we both entered his office.

He sat in a huge leather chair, behind a massive, elegant desk. To his left, in the corner, sat several thick, beautifully bound books.

I could see the title on them: "Svenska Lag" – Swedish Law.

He looked at me and asked:

> "Tell me, why are you applying for permanent residency in Sweden instead of Denmark, Finland, or Norway? Out of all the Scandinavian countries, why did you choose Sweden?"

I paused for a moment and then said:

> "Mr. Attorney, do you have time? To answer your question, I need to explain everything in detail so you can understand why Sweden."

He leaned back comfortably in his chair, ready to hear my story. After an hour and a half, I concluded by saying:

> *"This is my story."*

I had told him everything you've just read. I'd like to point out that nowadays, when young people hear the word story, they often think of fairy tales for children. But in my generation, a story meant real events that took place in one's life, not imagination.

He looked at me. I didn't know what was behind his eyes, but I saw no anger or hostility. He knew I had told him the whole truth. I was ready for whatever God had prepared for me. Suddenly, he placed his big left hand on several volumes of Swedish Law resting on his desk. Looking at me, he said:

> "This is Swedish Law. According to it, I handle cases for many people."

Then, he reached into his left pocket, near his heart, and pulled out a small book. Holding it up, he said:

> "And this is God's Law."

He pointed to a small New Testament.

> "I will do everything in my power to help you."

Tears filled my eyes. We said our goodbyes warmly. As I stepped out of the building, I realized that God had mixed up my appointment time, only so that, without my furious compatriot, I could tell my story in English, in my own words.

It was yet another miracle in my short life with God.

First, I was overwhelmed by immigration news. Then, the Bible school Dean was waiting for overdue payments. Now, my lawyer had to file an appeal. And suddenly, I was heading back to Sweden's eastern coast with joy in my heart.

Almost all my problems had been resolved, and once again, God's name was praised on my lips. He did it His way, not as I was thinking. God is good all the time!

After returning, I paid my school fees, passed my exams, and... what now? Should I enroll in the second year of Bible school, this time in Swedish?

My Swedish was getting better, after all, I was living among Swedes, though English was still dominant in my environment.

I fasted and prayed, not knowing what God had prepared for me. Then came the day when I received news that knocked me off my feet. No, it wasn't bad news, it was unbelievably good!

It turned out that the Swedish government had decided to grant amnesty or something along those lines. People who had arrived in Sweden before a certain date and had an open case in the immigration office were automatically granted permanent residence, regardless of whether their case was still pending or had been previously rejected.

Anyone reading my story might think I've lost my mind. You're absolutely right, one can go crazy with God's goodness!

We are not worthy of His help, and we don't deserve it. Yet, the verse that had always followed me manifested itself powerfully:

> "But seek first God's Kingdom and his righteousness;
> and all these things will be given to you as well."
>
> (WEB, Matthew 6:33)

Now I fully understood that when Wilma told me my case was resolved, it was resolved. My doubt, my sarcasm, all worth nothing.

To this day, I do not know how that humble woman had the courage to declare something only God knew about, something that was still in the future, something that no one else could have foreseen.

God, in His mercy, took away my fear, my sleepless nights, my nail-biting anxiety, and my sadness. He left me with indescribable joy and gratitude. What an amazing God I serve!

One day, I cried out:

> "Lord, I'm finishing school. I don't know what to do next. I no longer have to fear deportation. I have given You my life, please tell me what I should do next."

Suddenly, I heard one word:

> "Oslo".

I froze in place. Well, that was unexpected!

I began nurturing that word and saying:

CHAPTER 10 - PROVISION AND THE RED VOLVO

"God, I don't know what awaits me there, but I will go. I will drive toward Oslo."

I know, you probably think I've lost my mind, but what else could I do? I gave my life to God and said to Him:

"I accept everything You have for me. The only thing I have is my breath, my life. When I was driving my own life, I nearly destroyed it completely. Now You are my driver, and I am the passenger. If it's Oslo, then Oslo I will go!"

I went to the office where I worked delivering newspapers and announced that I was leaving for a mission to Oslo. I handed in my resignation and closed that chapter of my life.

At the restaurant where I worked, I told the owner that from that day forward, I could no longer work because I was leaving for a mission to Oslo.

He looked at me, stunned, he couldn't believe he was losing me as an employee. He asked:

"When will be your last day?"

And then he added:

"I would like to organize a farewell party for you."

A farewell party? For a young guy who washed dishes and pots? Yes, my dear friends. After lunch, they closed the restaurant, prepared a long table, filled it with food and drinks, and gave me a farewell party.

The restaurant owner said that after my first day of work, *(By the way, the day when I was wrestling with the Holy Spirit, thinking the devil was whispering to me that I shouldn't preach Jesus),* he called the entire restaurant team into the dish-washing area and said:

"I have never seen a dish-washing station this clean. It was so spotless, so organized, so pleasant that they

could have put a vase of flowers there and enjoyed a cup of coffee."

Everyone was amazed by the order and cleanliness of my workspace. Wow! I didn't expect that. Then they asked me:

"How did it happen that now you're going on a mission to Oslo?"

For over two hours, the entire restaurant staff sat at the table and listened to my testimony.

They were deeply moved by my story, and I, not even realizing it at first, saw God's hand in everything that had happened.

Instead of talking to them about Jesus during work, I worked as if for Jesus, doing my absolute best. My work was my testimony; it was a living Gospel among them. Now, for over two hours, I could freely share my life story and talk with them naturally, without interrupting work or having the boss complain that I wasn't doing my job.

God's hand was in all of this. And now, it was time to leave.

I canceled all my work contracts, ended my lease, packed my Volvo to the roof, and set off once again into the unknown, but this time, at God's call.

Believing He had things for me that I never even dreamed of... Or maybe, I had dreamed of them?

* * * * *

Chapter 11

The Road To Oslo

*A Journey of Faith and Miracles
and the fire that purifies faith.*

BACK THEN, THERE WAS NO such thing as a GPS. It was 1989. Maps lay on the passenger seat, next to a thermos of coffee and some sandwiches. I set out on a long journey to Oslo, driving my worn-out Volvo, with a heart full of anxiety, but also hope.

During my time at Bible school, one of the lecturers was an American, called Phil Driscoll. He taught us about worship. After he left, I spent my last savings on his cassette, "I Exalt Thee." I don't know if you can find it now, but your grandfather, then a young man, listened to that recording countless times. With tears streaming down my face, I drove toward Oslo.

You're probably wondering why I was crying. My dear ones, not long before that, I had stood on a highway, ready to throw myself under a truck.

Now I was driving to a city I didn't know, because the One who knows me through and through had answered my question,

"Lord, what should I do next?"

with a single word. I don't know if you can imagine it: driving such a long way into the unknown, simply because I believed I had heard God's voice. Of course, there were those who thought I was mentally ill.

My family had already written me off as crazy. I could count the critics of my decision by the handful. But what's better, to please people, or to please God?

They didn't save me when I stood at the crossroads of life. But He did. He said to me:

"You are loved, and you are needed."

Those words burned a mark into my heart, one I still cannot erase, extinguish, or deny. I was marked for life with a supernatural tattoo, invisible to the eye but heard in my voice every time I spoke to someone.

I didn't think twice about traveling from Sweden to Norway, even though my residency was only valid in Sweden. But more on that later.

After arriving in Oslo, I headed towards a large Christian church. Its name escapes me now, and I apologize to those I spoke with, but that's not the most important detail. Having already experienced sleeping in my car, the fear didn't seem so overwhelming.

During a Christian gathering, I shared my testimony. Someone passed it along, and that's how I ended up spending the night at the home of a church member, a young man on fire for God, who listened to my story with curiosity.

A few days later, I found myself in an Oslo Christian Radio Station. For two days, I was interviewed by the pastor who ran the station. I remember sitting with him in a small, glass-walled, soundproof room. In front of us stood a microphone with a black cover.

I asked him how he could speak to hundreds of thousands of people while sitting alone in that room.

He replied that every little hole in the microphone's cover represented a person listening to him.

With my broken English, I began to tell the story you've just read. The pastor asked questions, and I answered. Over the course of two days, I spent nearly eight hours in that studio, sharing what Jesus had done in my life.

At the end, he asked me to pray for the listeners. After a few minutes, we noticed that the people behind the glass had tears streaming down their faces. I asked what had happened. One of the staff members said they had received a phone call from a woman who, during the prayer, had placed her hand on a growth on her body, and the growth had fallen off onto the floor. A miracle. They confirmed it, sobbing.

On the way to my new friend's house, I cried with joy. I shouted in my car, because I had something called *"unspeakable joy."* You can't describe it with human words. You can only cry from happiness or go mad with joy. I began to cry out to the Lord:

> *"Now I know I was meant to come here. God, I need to find a job to support myself, and I will continue to preach Your Good News in Oslo."*

The next day, we went to a large park. We were talking while walking, until I noticed people in white shirts with black name tags, members of the Church of Jesus Christ of Latter-day Saints, formerly known as the Church of the Mormons until 2018. I listened to their conversations with strangers. I couldn't help myself; I shared my story. They stood frozen. They tried to steer the conversation their way, but who can change my testimony? It's physically impossible. At the beginning of my journey, I didn't speak Swedish, English, Danish, or Norwegian.

I didn't hear the Gospel flavored by their interpretations. I had a vision of my sinful life and a road leading straight to hell. No one could brainwash me with their ideas about faith.

I don't remember how that conversation ended, but I found myself standing in front of a building where people searched for jobs. There was no Internet back then, so I had to go in person to the Employment Office. I didn't find anything suitable, so I picked up a multi-page brochure with job listings. Tired from scanning the walls for postings, I finally opened the brochure, and suddenly, one offer seemed to rise off the page:

> *"English-speaking waiter needed for work on a passenger ship."*

At that moment, I remembered the vision I had had six months earlier. I knew this was the reason I had come to Oslo. I thought I would be preaching the Gospel in Norway, but God's ways are not our ways.

I asked my friend if I could use his phone to call the agent from the job listing. My prayer was fervent, passionate, full of faith. But I was missing one thing, a work permit for Norway.

The Employment Office told me I could obtain it at the police station. I went there immediately and presented my petition.

The officer looked me straight in the eye and said he could arrest me for being in Norway illegally.

If I didn't leave immediately, I would end up in jail. I walked out devastated. I hadn't anticipated this turn of events. I began to pray. I remembered the story of Smith Wigglesworth, a man who was illiterate, but after his conversion could read only the Holy Scriptures. Suddenly, I felt a surge of supernatural faith.

I stood in front of the police building and began to cry out:

> *"Devil, I have a message for you. You were defeated two thousand years ago on the cross by my Lord Jesus*

of Nazareth. You're finished. You're like a roaring lion, but without teeth. You can't touch me, because I am an ambassador of the Kingdom of God here on earth, not a refugee without papers. You tried to destroy me, but you failed. Now the One who is in me is stronger than you and all your demons. Who can be against me if God is with me? I speak to you in the authority of the Name of Jesus, the King of kings and Lord of Lords!"

I stomped my foot, as if crushing a yapping little dog under it. I believed the devil tucked his tail and ran off.

No one came out of the building. There was no earthquake. No one heard me, or maybe someone did. But inside me, faith rose. Faith like a mustard seed, the kind that moves mountains.

If God said "Oslo," then I am in Oslo!

I drove to the agent who had posted the job. I entered his large, elegant office, leather chairs, a massive desk, everything impressive.

I, a slender man, sat on the edge of one of the chairs. Opposite me sat a large, heavyset man. Compared to him, I looked like a comma in the sentence.

He began to question me. I presented my documents, translated into Swedish: my diploma from a culinary technical school, references from the finest hotel in Poznań, and certification as a master waiter. He looked at me and said:

"But you're from a communist country. Our ship is one of the most luxurious passenger vessels in the world.

We only hire staff from France, England, Austria, Germany, Switzerland, Italy. Why should I give this job to you?"

I calmly asked,

"Do you have time to hear my answer?"

He leaned back, lit a long cigar, and said,

"Go ahead."

"Sir, I need to say more than one sentence so you can have a full picture of who I am."

And so, for an hour and a half, I poured out my heart to this man. I told him why I believed this position was reserved by God specifically for me.

I don't know what you would have said if you had heard what he did, but even after four decades, I still remember his words:

"Hundreds of Norwegians applied for this job, but I don't know why... I have a feeling I should give it to you."

I replied calmly:

"Sir, this position is reserved for me by God." I won't be working for you; I work for the Lord Jesus. He sent me here. You'll see that I'll be the best employee you've ever had on that ship, because I work as unto God."

The agent was speechless. He hadn't expected such an answer. His secretary prepared a letter confirming my employment, which I needed to apply for a U.S. visa, since the ship would also dock in American ports. I didn't know what kind of ship it was, but I knew one thing, it was the ship from my dream, the vision I had six months earlier.

Now I began to understand why God had answered my prayer with just one word: *"Oslo."*

At the end of our meeting, the agent said,

"But please don't start a church on this ship."

I smiled and replied,

"Don't worry, it'll be OK."

There was one thing I deliberately left out during the interview: the full content of my vision.

I didn't want to freak him out by mentioning that I had seen the ship entering a hurricane, and I was the only person reaching out my hand to save others, shouting to them that Jesus would rescue them.

As I write these words, I feel compelled to share an observation. I've often heard people say:

"There's power in prayer."

But after much reflection, I've come to a different conclusion. I don't find that phrase explicitly confirmed in Scripture. What I do know is this, there is power in the One who hears our cries.

It's like someone praising the fork while enjoying a delicious meal. Instead of honoring the chef, their eyes are fixed on the utensil. The fork merely transfers the food from the plate to the mouth.

Prayer is just such a tool, it carries our cries, our tears, our groans to the ears of God Himself. When He responds, people say, *"There's power in prayer."* But I call it something else,

"it's the power of Almighty God".

I don't think I'm wrong. But I doubt I'll hear your counterarguments to this revelation. Now it's time for the next step in my journey, a direction completely different from what I had imagined.

Since I couldn't obtain a work permit in Norway, it turned out the agent had the option to employ me from within Swedish territory.

That complicated my situation a bit, but when God calls, He also equips. After all, I work as an ambassador of the Kingdom of God. Why would I panic? I remember how Matthew recorded the words of Jesus in his Gospel:

> "See the birds of the sky, that they don't sow, neither do they reap, nor gather into barns. Your heavenly Father feeds them. Aren't you of much more value than they? Which of you by being anxious can add one moment to his lifespan? Why are you anxious about clothing? Consider the lilies of the field, how they grow. They don't toil, neither do they spin, yet I tell you that even Solomon in all his glory was not dressed like one of these." (WEB, Matthew 6:26–29)

That's when I realized I needed to be saturated with God's Word, because it is life. It gives inspiration, It leads. So, I recalled another verse:

> "My people are destroyed for lack of knowledge." (WEB, Hosea 4:6)

Different Bible translations interpret *"lack of knowledge"* as a lack of spiritual understanding of God, which leads to drifting away from His commandments and law.

It's also ignorance that leads to sin and spiritual death; a lack of discernment between good and truth; a lack of wisdom and understanding that results in moral and spiritual collapse. That perfectly described my spiritual condition at that time when I had wanted to end my life.

Clearly, there are forces that truly desire our downfall.

Dear ones, if my closest family had already written me off, " the guy's gone mad", do you really think I'd be bothered by your opinion? Honestly, I couldn't care less. I've come to believe that no one cares about you as much as you do yourself.

And since I had discovered a treasure in my life, I decided to claim it and use it. God gave me a new life, but this time, it's not me who's behind the wheel; I am a passenger, or perhaps I should say that I try to be a passenger while the Holy Spirit is guiding.

I can already see some of your faces:

"Yep, he's lost it."

I wish everyone would "lose it" like that.

I pray you will experience what I did, because I still can't forget it, even after four decades. Instead of a tragic death, I now have a beautiful family, including grandchildren. And with all that, I have something to write about.

Let's keep going; this means the next step before setting sail into the unknown.

I had to return to Uppsala, and eventually I ended up in Stockholm, at the American embassy. By then, I already knew what my next step in life would be, after taking that first step of faith by going to Oslo.

I revisited some old friends who had once given me a roof over my head after spending several nights sleeping in my car, but I've written about that already.

When I shared with them the next steps I felt called to take, they looked at me with concern and said,

> *"That can't be from God. You, working on a ship as a waiter in a bar, serving alcohol to people? That's definitely not God's guidance."*

I tried to convince them that it was God who was sending me there. But they were older folks, prior missionaries in Tanzania, and they saw the world through a different lens.

So, I need to explain my point of view. Today, I understand people more than I used to. Those raised in a church-centered environment are like tomatoes in a greenhouse.

Everything is provided for them without effort: the right temperature, proper nutrients, light, and the removal of unnecessary offshoots that steal nourishment from the main stem.

> *(I know something about that, my mother's brother, Uncle Stefan, had several greenhouses, and as a child I helped him with tomatoes, carnations, begonias, cucumbers, strawberries...etc.)*

But dear ones, if that's how we define Christianity, then many people would never hear the Good News, the Gospel.

Christians would suffocate in their own aroma, by which I mean spiritual staleness, locked inside the four walls of a building, while people outside are dying from lack of knowledge about what Jesus has done for them.

It's like someone walking into a prison and proclaiming to the inmates:

> *"If you believe in the Only Begotten Son of God, Jesus, who died for you on the cross, and you turn away from your sinful life, confessing that He is the Lord of Lords, you will be free, saved, released from your symbolic cell."*

From what I've observed with my simple reasoning, because as you know, I'm a very simple man, many people are still sitting in their "spiritual cells" simply because no one has told them that all they need to do is turn the key and walk out into freedom.

I hope you understand me, in my simplicity.

If you still don't know what I'm writing about, then I beg you: go for a walk and start shouting:

> *"What is this man talking about? What is he writing?*
> *He's my father, my grandfather, my uncle, a stranger,*
> *but I don't get what he's saying!"*

I've come to the conclusion that those who call themselves Christians must engrave one truth deep into their hearts: they must become like children, just as Jesus said in Matthew 18:3

> "Most certainly I tell you, unless you turn and become as little children, you will in no way enter into the Kingdom of Heaven." (WEB, Matthew 18:3)

That means being humble, free from pride, trusting and open toward God. It means having a simple and sincere heart, rejecting calculation and self-reliance, and being ready to receive God's grace instead of depending on your own strength and abilities.

Until this truth is revealed to them, they will remain full of fear, unmoved and deceived, and they will never truly understand what happened when they confessed their sins, turned away from a sinful life, and were baptized. They don't realize that baptism was a declaration, to God, to angels, to demons, and to the devil himself, that they died with Jesus in that water and were resurrected into new life when they came out of it.

Yes, I'm talking about water baptism, in case that wasn't clear. After that moment, you need to know you became a new, powerful offspring with the privilege of calling yourself a "Child of God"

So often I hear on TV programs and in casual conversations the phrase, "We're all God's children."

And I almost want to shout, "NO! Don't deceive your listeners, because that's simply not true." God created all of us, yes, but He gave us free will. Otherwise, we'd be like robots.

And you can't expect love from a robot, only from someone who can choose to love freely.

> "But as many as received Him, to them He gave the right to become God's children, to those who believe in His name." (WEB, John 1:12)

> "In this the children of God are revealed, and the children of the devil. Whoever doesn't do righteousness is not of God, neither is he who doesn't love his brother." (WEB, 1 John 3:10)

> "For as many as are led by the Spirit of God, these are children of God." (WEB, Romans 8:14)

Dear ones, please remember, not all people are children of God. Only those who have believed, been born of God, and received Christ as Savior and Lord become His children.

That's the sting of this lesson.

Now I will continue with my story about what happened next.

After visiting the American embassy in Stockholm, I had to sell my old Volvo, because now I was switching to a water-bound machine, and I had no idea what would come next. Edwin helped me sell the car immediately for cash, and with part of the money I was able to buy a plane ticket to fly back to Oslo.

I don't remember exactly when I was supposed to report to the ship, but I still had some time to sort out my affairs and prepare for a new chapter in my life.

To all those who say, or believe, that life with God is boring, I can only say:

"you have absolutely no idea".

I'm not talking about religious orders or monasteries.

I'm talking about walking with the living God and not being immersed in the traditions created by man.

One day I'll speak more boldly on this topic, but for now I'll keep moving, otherwise I'll never finish this book.

Chapter 12

Seabourn Pride: A Mission At Sea

A luxury ship, a divine assignment,
and a storm that tested both.

WITH THE LAST BIT OF money, I had before boarding the ship that was to depart from the port in Oslo, I had to buy white shoes. I must say, Norway isn't exactly a country where white leather shoes are in high demand. Summer is relatively short compared to southern countries. But despite my financial situation, I bought a beautiful pair of white shoes. I said goodbye to my friends and headed to the port to see the ship from my vision.

Wow! It was called Seabourn Pride, you could translate that as "Pride born on the sea." My jaw dropped. I had never seen anything like it.

I'd only heard of the Polish passenger ship Batory, named after Stefan Batory, but this one was modern, stunning, and intimidating.

After boarding, I was led to the appropriate person who issued me my uniform and assigned me a temporary cabin. I had no idea what kind of ship this was. Back then we didn't have smartphones to go online and check everything instantly.

145

In my spirit, I prayed that I'd remember the way from the crew mess to my cabin. As you can imagine, there was some fear, but everyone has to go through that. No one is born and raised on a ship.

I should mention that my English was primarily biblical. I knew the meanings of many theological terms as I was a freshly appointed ambassador of the Kingdom of God, and I had learned the language on my knees, praying daily with a Polish/English dictionary. I never attended an English course or school. I preached to everyone I met as best I could. I read theological books with a dictionary, wrote Polish translations under each sentence, and did everything I could to make it work.

And now I found myself in the belly of the beast, my new place of residence.

That evening in the cabin, after receiving my uniforms and everything I needed to function, I sat down with Stuart.

He was from Scotland, around 35 years old, and it turned out he was my manager. He oversaw four bars and supervised the wine stewards in the main dining room.

We sat together, and suddenly he said, *"I'm gay."*

I replied, *"I'm Jacek."*

He was stunned. He repeated, *"I'm gay."*

I said, *"OK, I'm Jacek."*

Eventually, he realized I didn't understand what he was trying to tell me, so he said, *"I'm homosexual."*

"Aha," I replied. And in that moment, I clenched my buttocks and said to myself, *"Well, this is going to be interesting."*

> *(I had learned English on my own, on my knees with a Polish-English dictionary as my only light in prayer. The word "gay" didn't exist in my world, and that's why I couldn't understand that he was talking about his orientation.)*

The first night, I'm in a cabin with my manager, who immediately informs me that he's homosexual.

The light went out in the cabin, time to sleep, and suddenly a conversation began, unlike any I'd had before. As you might expect, I told him how I ended up on this ship.

My whole testimony, short version. He turned the light back on. I sat on the bunk bed, and he asked me a question with fear in his eyes:

"Who sent you here?"

I replied:

"Jesus."

I continued sharing my story, and suddenly he said:

"You weren't sent here by my family."

I couldn't believe what I was hearing. He told me I spoke exactly like his aunt, his mother's sister, who lives either in the USA or Canada.

I told him I had no idea what he meant, but I said,

"Stuart, I will pray for you."

He went on to say that his aunt had a vision and told his mother that something was wrong with Stuart. At the time, no one knew he was gay.

Dear ones, that first night I won over my manager, who, from the very beginning, recognized something in me. I must admit, even though I was young, handsome, and athletic, he never made any advances towards me.

He was always respectful, something I can't say about everyone else. The first days were the hardest: getting to know all the decks, bars, restaurants, and crew areas. Ten hours of work a day, every day. It turns out that after six months, you absolutely need to take a vacation to rest.

I remember taking an order from a heavyset American. Most of the people we had on board were wealthy like him. He was from Texas, and when I asked what he'd like to drink, he replied:

"Stin...er."

I went to the bartender and, just like my guest, I croaked out:

"Stin...er."

The bartender, a Frenchman, Pierre, asked me:

"What is that?"

Again, I said:

"Stin...er."

"What is that?" he grumbled, already annoyed.

"I don't know," I said. *"That's what he ordered."*

"Go ask him what it is."

Not an easy thing to ask a guest what he meant, especially when we're working on the most luxurious ship in the world.

The guest replied:

"You don't know what a Stin...er is?" "No, sir,"

I answered. *"Brandy and white creme de menthe."*

I went back to the bartender and told him what it was.

"Aah, Stinger!" "Well, that's what I said, Stin...er."

It makes me laugh that I still remember that moment nearly 36 years later. I used to go to bed with a Bible and a book about drinks. I had no idea there were so many kinds of alcohol.

Now I know that a Stinger is an after-dinner drink, served mostly among the upper classes, especially in the 1920s. You might say:

"So that's the kind of mission you landed on, serving alcohol to people. Not very noble."

Dear ones, I wasn't sent there to convert those people, I was sent to save them from the hurricane I saw in my vision.

I didn't share these things with the crew, because they'd probably have thrown me overboard.

"Crazy, possessed, out of his mind, we need to get rid of him."

We sailed through Scandinavia, up to the North Pole, then the Baltic Sea and all the coastal ports: Leningrad Russia (as it was then), Finland, Hamburg (West Germany), France, Spain, the Riviera, Italy, Greece, the Corinth Canal, all the way to Israel.

Back then, we had bomb alerts on board because we were in regions not very friendly to Americans and Israelis.

In Israel, I walked the Via Dolorosa, "Sorrowful Way"; the street where Jesus carried the cross to Golgotha, and "The Wailing Wall" and so on.

It was an incredible experience to stand on the stones where the Lord Jesus had walked over 2,000 years ago.

I walked the streets of Jerusalem, seeing squads of young soldiers running in groups with rifles slung over their shoulders. Jews of all kinds: with side locks, different hats, everything you can imagine.

Then came Egypt. On the ship was a Travel Manager who invited me to fly with him to Giza, where the pyramids and the Sphinx were, to help him organize passengers for flights or hotels.

I don't know why he chose me, but I was the only crew member who flew over the Sahara desert to that place.

Of course, I saw many historic sites, you know what I mean. And if not, go watch some online videos about the pyramids and the Sphinx.

After dinner, we landed at the hotel. Tired, we showered and jumped into bed, because early in the morning we were heading to the next location, where we had to watch over the passengers.

And suddenly, the Travel Manager climbs into my bed and cuddles up to me. I froze. I turned around and said:

"What are you doing, man?" "I'm not homosexual!"

And he said: *"I thought you were."*

He got out of my bed, and I prayed in my heart, crying out to God to help me restrain myself from beating him up.

You may remember, I was a bit crazy when it came to hand-to-hand combat. I really didn't want to hurt him out in the desert far from the ship. It was hard to fall asleep.

I was deeply shocked. I know, I was a handsome, young guy: always clean shaven, with a little mustache, smelling of good aftershave. Was that why that man thought I was one of his kind? After all, I couldn't work behind the bar with dirty fingernails, greasy hair, unshaven, and with my hair blown by the wind on deck. Maybe I should have smelled of sweat so that no one would come near me. Total absurdity.

I'm writing about this because I'll refer to it again later.

We returned to the ship, but that situation stayed with me. We never had a face-to-face encounter again. I think he realized how inappropriate his behavior was toward me.

Months passed, but I must mention that every time the sea was rough, and the waves crashed against the bow so hard that water splashed onto the highest deck, the Sky Bar, I would quietly step outside. No one was there, because normal people were hiding in their cabins and lounges, or hugging a toilet!

But I would shout into the wind, commanding it to change direction, for the sea to calm down, in the Powerful Name of Jesus.

I didn't know when the vision I had would come to pass, so I was always ready for action. It makes me laugh, because I can see your faces and hear the words:

"This guy is nuts. He's totally lost it."

You're absolutely right. I was totally ready to save the people on that ship.

A little question: if you were on such a ship, not knowing that someone was there watching over you, praying for your well-being, would you prefer that he be there, crying out to God for help, or would you rather experience the Titanic firsthand?

Exactly. The answer is simple. However crazy it looked, I believe the angels were watching me and saying:

"He really believes in what he saw in the vision."

"Lord, we've got someone who believes in what You showed him. The day will come when he passes the test."

Weeks and months passed, and I, who once told God I wanted to be like the Apostle Paul, without marital or family obligations, fully devoted to serving Him, began to sigh in my prayers, saying,

"Lord, forget my earlier prayers. I need a wife to help me in every area of my life."

Surely the heavens smiled and said:

"Finally, he's matured enough to start a family."

I was nearly 29 at the time. My father always repeated the saying:

"Unmarried by thirty, not wealthy by forty, a beggar by fifty."

Well, he unknowingly instilled that in me so deeply that the approaching thirty felt like a door I had to pass through and not be late.

Work wasn't easy, but I saw a good chunk of the world.

The passengers were mostly American businessmen, some rotten to the core. It became necessary to take a vacation just to avoid killing the people we had to smile at seven days a week, 24 hours a day.

I started as a bar waiter and a wine steward, and the next promotion was supposed to be bartender. After about seven months, I had to take a break. We were sailing along the western coast of the U.S. from Los Angeles or San Francisco to Acapulco, Mexico.

When we arrived in Acapulco, I used my free time to reserve a small, cheap hotel room for when I'd return on vacation.

I didn't want to go back to Europe, because it was winter there, and we mostly sailed in warm climates year-round.

After disembarking in Los Angeles, I took a taxi, probably rode for an hour. The driver spoke Russian, and I was able to show off my Russian skills with him. He kept advising me not to go to downtown L.A. I didn't understand why he repeated it so many times, but... Well, I ended up there with a small bag, the rest I'd left on the ship. I started exploring, step by step, and found myself on a big street.

It was evening, lots of lights, and I was wearing a black leather jacket, a gold chain on my wrist, $5,000 in my pocket, and a Canon camera slung over my shoulder. I probably looked like a walking ATM.

But I walked on, praying in my spirit: "If God is with me, who can be against me?"

Today, as I write this, I'm amazed at how bold, or maybe reckless, I was. Dear ones, remember in the army I could fight six opponents at once, so I wasn't afraid. I was confident I could handle any punk who tried to attack me. I really wanted to see the new movie, "The Best of the Best" an American martial arts film; it was 1989. I found a cinema on that big street.

All the other stores had their metal anti-theft shutters down, but I decided to go in. The movie was about to start. I bought a ticket and two Snickers bars, gave a tip to the guy who sold them, and noticed he looked at me like I'd dropped in from the moon.

It was drizzling outside, so I figured it was a good time to avoid walking in the rain. When I entered the theater, I realized I was the only white person in the audience.

It makes me laugh now; I must've looked ridiculous in their eyes. I had no idea I was in a black neighborhood, and that white people just didn't do things like that.

I left the cinema, the movie was excellent, and my stomach started growling, so I decided to hop into a McDonald's.

Dear ones, I'd never been to McDonald's before. In Poland, we didn't have one. In Sweden, I never had the money to eat in places like that.

Now, being on the ship and having cash in my pocket, I felt a bit of freedom, that I could go to a place like that and grab something quick to eat. Reminder: this was a black neighborhood. I walked in, and there was a line. People looked at me, I was dressed decently, well-groomed, and here I was, a lone White guy among Black Americans, late at night. I didn't see anything wrong with it, but I remembered the taxi driver's warning: *"Don't go to downtown L.A."*

Too late, I was already there. I stood in front of the menu board, wondering what to order. After getting my food, I sat at a table. People stared at me like I was from another planet.

Then suddenly, a young man, maybe a bit younger than me, approached and asked if I had a quarter to spare. I'd just looked at the menu and knew you couldn't buy anything for 25 cents.

So, under the table, I pulled out a wad of American bills. He didn't see how much I had, and I gave him five dollars. When he saw that, he started thanking me profusely and asked where I was from.

He was shocked that someone had given him that much money without hesitation. And you can imagine your crazy grandpa started  telling him how I'd been homeless in Copenhagen, how I'd wanted to end my life, and how my journey unfolded. I saw tears welling up in that young man's eyes. I took his hands right there in front of the other customers and began to pray for him. I left full and deeply satisfied by what had happened there.

Evening had fallen, it was dark, and about 50 meters away I saw two shady-looking guys. I had a bad feeling. I walked quickly until I saw a sign: "Hotel."

The person behind the glass window, when I asked if they had any rooms, replied: *"Show me the cash."* I showed him $100, and he asked where I was from.

I said I was from Europe and flying to Mexico tomorrow. I got a room. I don't remember how much it cost, but I was glad it had a door I could lock and a bed to sleep in after my wandering through downtown L.A.

The reason I had to spend a day in Los Angeles was that, after disembarking from my ship and heading to the airport to travel to Mexico, the lady at the check-in counter asked me for a visa. I opened my eyes wide. I had no idea that, as a Polish citizen, I needed a visa to enter Mexico. I thought my passport would be enough. It turned out that Mexico required a visa from citizens of my communist homeland.

This whole mess forced me to make a morning visit to the Mexican embassy in LA to purchase an entry visa.

In the morning, after a night's sleep, I set out for the embassy, but first I stepped into a nearby restaurant.

I hadn't realized that I had ended up in a district full of Asian restaurants and boutiques.

I had never been to a Chinese restaurant before, so when I looked at the menu, I didn't understand a thing. To me, it was all "Chinese", meaning, in slang, nobody knows what's going on.

I glanced at the prices in dollars and pointed to a few dishes. The waitress, speaking broken English worse than mine, asked if I was expecting someone else. I said no. From her expression, I sensed something was off.

After a few minutes, my table was overflowing with dishes. I thought everything was cheap, so I ordered without hesitation, not realizing these were American portions.

If you don't know what an "American portion" is, it's enough to feed our entire communist family: parents plus two kids, all together.

After that curious event, I went to the embassy. I thought the story would end with a flight to Mexico, but no, I have to tell you, I was shocked. I saw people sleeping in cardboard boxes, homeless people on every corner. Every few steps, someone asked me for money. I was stunned that in such a powerful country, there were so many poor, dirty, foul-smelling people that it made my nose twist. But what can you expect here? Everyone is free!!

Yet freedom without boundaries can cause a person to fall out of the "box of life" and end up on the street.

I understand that some people are mentally ill, but seeing healthy individuals, my brain was burning with questions and I had no one to ask.

Years later, I understood, Los Angeles is in California, and California is a world of its own. Californians are different Americans. It's a whole other reality.

I arrived at the airport and after a few hours of flight the doors opened, and a wave of humid hot air hit my face. Welcome to Mexico, Acapulco!

I checked into a hotel, but after two nights I looked for another, because the first one didn't feel safe. The next one was more expensive, but I figured it was better to spend more than risk my life for a few dollars.

> *I found a beach and spent countless hours there. I must confess, especially to my children and grandchildren, that this was your beginning.*

You might ask, *"Grandpa, we weren't born in Mexico?"* My dear ones, every day, from morning till evening, I lay on the beach with my Bible beside me. I read it, prayed, and cried out for a wife, for a whole month.

I knew that God is a God of order. If I was going to ask Him for something, I had to know what I wanted. If He placed a woman in front of me who was six feet five inches tall, I'd look like her son. If she weighed 300 pounds, I'd look like a comma in a sentence.

So I prayed with details: that she would be English-speaking (American or British), so I wouldn't have to pay for English lessons.

I wanted her to be blonde, shorter than me, but not too short, proportionate, and pretty in the face, so I wouldn't be ashamed to walk with her or introduce her to my family.

> *"Grandpa, you're such a character! You're bothering God with things like that!"*

You might think. But knowing God's word, I read:

> "Which of you fathers, if your son asks for bread, will give him a stone? Or if he asks for a fish, will give him

a serpent instead of a fish? Or if he asks for an egg, will
give him a scorpion?" (WEB, Luke 11:11–12)

To me, that was proof that God, as a good Father, gives good things to those who ask Him. I prayed for 30 days.

In the Gospel of Luke, Jesus says:

"Ask, and it will be given to you. Seek, and you will find. Knock, and it will be opened to you. For everyone who asks receives. He who seeks finds. To him who knocks it will be opened." (WEB, Luke 11:9–10)

So, I knocked on His proverbial door day and night, because I didn't want to be alone. I was ready to start a family.

The sun burned me so badly that I developed little white bumps, it could've been sunburn, an inflammatory reaction, or photo-dermatitis. But they disappeared after I limited my sun exposure for a few days.

One day, craving something green, I ordered a salad. The next day, I wanted to go to the beach, but suddenly I felt something happening in my stomach. I rushed back to the hotel, nothing came out, but the feeling was awful. I tried again to go to the beach, and again the same terrible sensation.

This time, I grabbed my Polish/English dictionary and looked up the word "diarrhea." I found it but couldn't pronounce it. So, I took the dictionary with me and went to a pharmacy.

I stood in line and shyly pointed to the word. The pharmacist nodded and gave me tablets. What a relief!

Just a side note, remember tap water, ice, and salad in Mexico are a big No. No!!! Our bodies aren't ready for the bacteria they have in their water and leafy greens. Week after week passed. My ship returned to port, I dropped off souvenirs, picked up new clothes, and showed off my tan to my coworkers. I forgot to tell you that my new contract was already signed; I was going to become a bartender.

Promotion! The manager said I was the best bar waiter, and now I was stepping up to bartender.

The ship sailed away, and I remained: beach, prayer, Bible, and counting down the days until my return to Los Angeles.

The day of departure arrived, and I must admit, I had had enough of Acapulco after four weeks.

Burned mahogany-brown by the sun, I looked like a local Mexican, my complexion dark and weathered.

Upon landing in Los Angeles, it was time to go through immigration, and suddenly, I hit a wall.

> *"Visa? What's the purpose of your stay in the U.S.?" they asked. I replied, "I work on a cruise ship." But they said, "Sir, you don't have a work visa."*

I froze. *"Here we go,"* I thought. I began praying in the Spirit, rebuking every force of darkness in the name of Jesus. And then, just a few meters away, some fellow crew members from my ship were passing by. Hearing my interrogation, they shouted,

> *"Let him through! He's with us on the ship!"*, and something else I didn't quite catch.

Suddenly, as if by divine intervention, the officer stamped my Polish passport, and my feet once again stood on American soil.

I checked into a hotel, then returned to the port, back in familiar surroundings, but this time I was dressed in my new bartender uniform. I was assigned to the Club Bar, which also housed a small casino and a piano that played beautiful melodies for passengers before and after dinner. The bar closed around three or four in the morning.

I shared a cabin with Diddier, from the French-speaking part of Switzerland. He would wake up an hour after I returned to serve pastries and coffee at the Sky Bar for the EMR, Early Morning Risers.

We passed each other like ships in the night. I slept while he worked.

Weeks passed, and the time came to sail from the West Coast of the U.S. and Mexico through the Panama Canal to the Caribbean.

The crew always threw a farewell party to celebrate the end of one route and the beginning of another.

A few days before that event, I went to the crew mess for dinner, and there, unexpectedly, she appeared.

A beautiful woman entered the small room with a TV mounted above the crew's dining table. My jaw dropped. I was speechless. I shyly struck up a conversation. She was from England, shorter than me, with bleached blonde hair, everything in the right place, and her weight just right. English was her native language.

After a brief chat, she walked off in her own direction. She worked in the beauty salon as a massage therapist and was also the fitness director for the passengers. I returned to my bar, but I couldn't get her out of my mind.

Yes, my dear ones, I began to pray.

"God, give me a sign. Is she the one?"

But nothing came. Silence on the heavenly line. So, I kept praying. Meanwhile, I should mention, almost everyone on board knew my story. They knew that if they started talking to me, the conversation would end up being about Jesus. So, among themselves, they gave me the nickname *"Jesus."*

I didn't know about it until someone I trusted told me. I had never had a nickname like that before. Considering how I used to live and behave, *"Devil"* would have been far more fitting.

But since the day I asked Jesus for help, my sinful life collapsed like a house of cards, and I was completely transformed.

One day, a wealthy Canadian woman sat at the bar and ordered a drink.

You know how it is at the bar; people have nothing else to do but talk about the sea, the ports, and watch others. Hearing my foreign accent, she began to question me, friendly and curious.

Like a bull in a China shop, I started telling her how I ended up on the ship, carefully avoiding the tragedy that was about to unfold, and there behind the bar, the woman began to cry.

She asked me who I was, because something was happening inside her as I spoke. I don't think the drink I made had those properties, but before every shift, I always prayed:

*"Lord, bring me someone new today with whom
I can share what You've done in my life."*

Every two weeks, we had new passengers, fresh blood, so I never lacked opportunities to talk. Eventually, they asked me questions, so I didn't have to try too hard to start conversations.

I asked for this woman, now in tears, her mascara running down her face, for her name. Standing behind the bar, I quietly began to pray for her. I didn't want to cause a scene, but I could see the Holy Spirit was touching her in a tangible way.

Suddenly, my manager appeared behind me and asked what was going on. But knowing who I was, he left me alone.

I was simply serving a woman who was drowning her sorrows at the bar. To my old friends who once told me this job wasn't from God, I don't know what they'd say about that moment.

I've never seen healthy people sitting in a doctor's waiting room. That's why I fully agree with what Jesus said:

"Those who are healthy have no need for a physician, but those who are sick do. I came not to call the righteous, but sinners to repentance."   (WEB, Mark 2:17)

Jesus also said:

> "Behold, I send you out as sheep among wolves. Therefore, be wise as serpents, and harmless as doves."
>
> WEB, Matthew 10:16)

This verse reminds me that He instructed His disciples to be both wise and shrewd like serpents, and pure and blameless like doves, as they went out to preach the Gospel in a hostile world.

My world was my workplace. Remember, I told the recruiting agent that I work as if for the Lord Jesus, not for him and I wanted to remain faithful to that mission.

The only thing I was waiting for was a proper storm, so I could redirect the winds and save that ten-thousand-ton vessel on turbulent waters.

I could write another book just about my conversations with the crew and passengers but let me move on to more important matters. Not to diminish those conversations in the slightest, but I want to tell you that my time on the ship felt like sitting in a chair, ready to rise and step into action.

Now back to the farewell party at the stern of the ship.

Midnight was approaching, nearly everything was closed, except the Club Bar, where I had the day off. I searched everywhere for the woman I had met days earlier in the crew mess. She wasn't there.

I checked every corner of the ship's rear deck. She had vanished like vapor. All I could do was pray that she would appear again, and that I might get to know her better. I believe God planted something in my heart that I couldn't shake.

My grandmother used to say that love is worse than diarrhea, you never know when it'll hit you again!

Dear ones, at that time, the woman who had just joined our ship, who had been sent by a company that placed staff on various cruise lines, was lying in her bed, tossing and turning, unable to sleep.

She knew there was a crew party happening, but she didn't know anyone and didn't want to go. Meanwhile, I was storming the heavens, searching for her everywhere, not knowing which cabin was hers.

Suddenly, she got up, got dressed, and walked out onto the deck, without knowing why.

I must tell you while I was praying, very specifically, in Mexico for a wife, she was working on another ship.

She always had nine-month contracts, and this was her third contract. So, she was surprised when, after just a month on one ship, she was transferred to another, and then again after one more month relocated to my ship!

Don't tell me prayer has power? I've already explained that power belongs to God the Father, who hears our cries and chooses whether to answer or not.

Sometimes it's better if He doesn't answer, because our prayers can be foolish, impulsive, and poorly thought out. But that's beside the point.

She landed on my ship, and now, at midnight, someone in the spiritual realm nudged her to go out on deck, where I was scanning the horizon like an eagle waiting for its prey.

Suddenly, she appeared. Without hesitation, I walked briskly up to her and offered her a drink.

I started talking to her in my peculiar English, broken, in her opinion, peppered with theological expressions she didn't understand.

When I saw the puzzled look on her face, I asked if she knew what I meant. So, imagine this: until four in the morning, nearly four hours, I told her my whole life story. She looked at me like the kind of man her mother had warned her about, a fanatic, probably in some cult. But at the end, I said:

> *"If tomorrow, just a few hours from now, you greet me with a smile, we can be friends."*

Poor thing probably couldn't sleep after hearing my conversion testimony. I went back to my cabin and began to pray.

> *"Lord, is this really the woman I've been praying for? I don't want to make a mistake."*

Silence. I kept knocking on heaven's door and suddenly, I heard a familiar voice:

> *"Yes, she is the one."*

I rejoiced for a split second, until a verse flashed before my eyes.

> "Don't be unequally yoked with unbelievers, for what fellowship do righteousness and iniquity have? Or what fellowship does light have with darkness?"
>
> (WEB, 2 Corinthians 6:14)

I cried out bitterly,

> *"Lord, what about this verse? From our conversation, she's not a believer like I am."*

Immediately, I heard the reply,

> *"I'm giving her into your hands."*

I was stunned. I'd heard other Christians preach moral lessons about how this couldn't possibly be from God. I swallowed hard and said:

> *"Lord, thank You for hearing my cry. Now it's time for me to do everything I can to help her become like me, so we can pull this wagon of life together, as one kind of ox or donkey."*

Now, I won't speak for the ox, but my future wife, who had no idea about my intentions, was stubborn like a donkey, not an ox. But those are her words, not mine, so don't accuse me of insulting anyone. Her name was Wendy.

And so, my next mission began preaching the Gospel to this pagan woman from the Anglican Church, which, according to her, meant absolutely nothing.

Again, those are her words, not mine, so hold your judgments.

She had only ever been to church for weddings and funerals.

She knew nothing about the Resurrection of Jesus, which is the foundation of Christianity. She thought Easter was a holiday all about devouring fancy chocolate eggs from a bunny!

OK, I won't go into more detail about what she did or didn't know. I prayed and worked on winning her heart.

After a week, I told her I had serious intentions towards her. She, in her heart, thought we could be friends, but nothing more.

She later told me that at first, she thought I was too polite, too kind, too clean, too skinny and used way too much hairspray! She thought I was gay! ...which I was definitely not!!

But all her thoughts, of which I had no idea, didn't shake me, because I had a Word from the Lord that she would be my wife.

Her birthday was approaching, so I went to the ship's store, where you could buy all sorts of interesting items, and I bought her a rather elegant bracelet.

When I gave it to her, she said:

"I can't accept this." But I insisted.

"We don't know each other well enough for you to give me such expensive gifts," she said.

My reply was immediate:

"My dear, don't worry, I'm not losing anything. I'm investing in our future together."

Poor girl didn't know what to do with me.

Once I found out where her cabin was, I started bringing her cappuccino and fresh Danish pastries in the morning before work. In the evenings, we'd sit at the back of the ship during sunset, enjoying fresh baguette with French cheese and sipping wine.

And I'd tell her, at every opportunity, about my adventures in Sweden, Norway, on the ship, in the U.S., in Russia, Poland and so on.

One time, we planned to go horseback riding in the Dominican Republic. Along with a few other crew members, we set off inland to ride, but it didn't happen. We ended up in a poolside bar. To order a drink, you had to step into the pool and walk up to the bar counter. Time passed, and I had to return to work on the ship.

Wendy and the others stayed by the pool. Suddenly, I walked up to Wendy, who was lying on a deck chair with her eyes closed, and kissed her on the lips. It was a bold move, but I wanted her to know I was head over heels in love.

She froze. In her heart, she thought, *"What are you doing?"*

But she said nothing. She was probably so shocked by the kiss that she lost her breath and couldn't speak.

And me? It was like I'd been injected with adrenaline; I rushed back to the ship full of joy and optimism.

Dear ones, your grandpa was once young and wild too. Don't look at me now and think I've always been the same. I used to wear hair gel, cologne, and stylish clothes. I wanted to look sharp so Wendy wouldn't be ashamed of me. I laugh as I write this, because I remember standing at the back of the ship on the crew deck, dressed in a yellow short-sleeved shirt with palm trees, yellow pants, and yellow leather shoes.

Wendy walked up to me, we'd known each other a bit longer by then, and she ripped off my yellow shirt and threw it overboard. I'm laughing out loud writing this. I thought I looked fabulous, all matching colors, and she told me that I looked like a gay man.

OK, so I had to change. Guys were drawn to me like bees to honey, or flies to.... Well, you know!

Months passed, and Wendy began to melt like butter in the sun. We crossed the Atlantic again, arriving in London, under the London Bridge, on her home turf.

We were finally in Europe. Wendy's family was coming aboard, her father, mother, and sisters. So, I prepared canapes, champagne, and asked my Polish friend from Australia, an officer responsible for supplies, to help me get ready for something Wendy had no idea about.

When they boarded, we invited them to a beautiful officer's cabin with a view of London Bridge. I walked up to Wendy's father, looked him straight in the eye, and said:

"Mr. Wheadon, I'd like to ask you, in the presence of your family, for your daughter's hand in marriage."

Everyone froze. Wendy said, *"But you haven't asked me!"*

I replied, *"Wendy, your hand belongs to your father as the head of your household. So, I'm officially asking him for permission."*

Her mother and sisters were so moved I swear it had started raining inside the cabin. It was a moment I'll never forget, and I doubt anyone who witnessed it will either. Yes, of course, I got Mr. Wheadon's blessing. But only the hand. The rest, I had to fight for much longer.

After crossing the Atlantic, we set out on our next journey, this time toward Norway and the Baltic Sea. In Oslo, I had the opportunity to meet again with the agent who had given me the chance to work on this ship. You won't believe it; he was thrilled by what he'd heard about me from my superiors.

It had been nearly three months since I became a bartender. One day, I was summoned to the office of the hotel director on-board, who also oversaw all the bars. Looking me in the eye, he asked a question I'll never forget:

"Do you know 150 people like yourself?"

I replied:

"I'm sorry, I don't understand the question."

He said:

"You're the kind of employee we wish everyone on this ship could be."

He must've heard about me from my manager and the agent who hired me. Not a single passenger complained about me. In short, I was a well-liked crew member.

At the end of the meeting, he said:

"Starting tomorrow, you'll be the manager of all four bars. You'll also oversee the wine steward in the dining room, train new bar waiters and bartenders, wine stewards, create work schedules for everyone in the bars, and we hope you'll manage well.

I must admit, I was completely surprised by this promotion. Nine months earlier, I had started at the lowest position, and now I was the manager of the entire bar operation. I got to work.

Some people were upset that I had been chosen as their boss, especially since they had been bartenders when I first joined the ship, but after nine months of hard work, I was now their leader.

Dear friends, as I wrote earlier, I told the agent that I don't work for him, but for the Lord Jesus.

After a few weeks, those who had been angry with me gave me a gift to apologize. They saw that I was doing a great job and hadn't let the promotion go to my head. I still did my best to make sure everyone was satisfied. I worked 12 hours a day, because my responsibilities had grown significantly.

What I want to add and encourage you with, is this, whatever you do in life, remember that God sees you. When we humble ourselves, He lifts us up.

I wasn't wise enough to do that on my own, but God's Word served it to me on a platter.

> "For everyone who exalts himself will be humbled,
> and whoever humbles himself will be exalted."
>
> (WEB, Luke 14:11)

What more can I say? It's good to know God's mysteries, which are available to anyone who begins to seek them.

As I've written before, my people perish for lack of knowledge, for lack of understanding, for lack of God's instruction on how to live on this planet called Earth.

Wendy would sometimes say to me,

> "Can we talk about something else? You only talk about Jesus." I would reply, "But what's more important than Him?"

I understood, she wanted to talk about things that interested her. But I was so fascinated by Jesus, and I had no one else to share my discoveries with. Most people avoided me because they knew they'd get a dose of the Gospel.

Today I know it is necessary to feed people in small slices, not shove the whole salami into their mouths. But I was so excited about the things of God that my joy knew no bounds.

One day, I gathered the courage to tell Wendy my secret. The reason I was on this ship was I had seen it entering a hurricane at sea, and I was the one praying for the people onboard, asking God to save them from disaster. I told her that when the sea was raging, I would go out on deck and rebuke the wind, commanding the waters to be still, just as Jesus did:

> "He awoke, and rebuked the wind, and said to the sea, 'Peace! Be still!' The wind ceased, and there was a great calm." (WEB, Mark 4:39)

That event took place on the Sea of Galilee, when Jesus was asleep in the boat and a storm threatened the lives of His disciples.

So, I practiced my faith, because I didn't know when my day would come. (OK, I hear nothing from you, keep your judgments to yourselves.)

She looked at me with wide eyes, not knowing whether to laugh or cry.

This wasn't a joke, hearing such things while on the open ocean, with no other ships nearby and the waters raging. If it's true, it's not something to laugh about.

Days passed, and still nothing. We were crossing the Atlantic again. There was nothing to watch on the ship's TV screens, back then, you could only rent VHS tapes and watch movies to kill the boredom of being at sea.

What I'm describing is Wendy's experience. She had heard so much from me that she probably started praying out of fear, not for a revelation of who God is.

She sat on her bed and began searching for a channel on the TV. As I mentioned earlier, there's nothing out there on the open ocean. But suddenly, for a few seconds, a preacher appeared on the screen, saying things similar to what she'd heard from me.

She thought, *"This is impossible!"*

It was a divine sign in her life, that besides me, there were others saying the same things. She needed confirmation that I wasn't a lunatic, but a follower of Jesus, like many others on this Earth.

To confirm what you're about to read, I want to emphasize that I had reached the highest position I could in my profession.

I was good at it, praised by my boss, and there was no reason to give up such a role.

People would've loved to work on the most luxurious ship in the world at that time, traveling the globe and earning money they could save entirely, since we had free housing, meals, and laundry.

To live and not die, as my grandmother Wanda used to say.

I don't remember the exact month or day, but I remember clearly what happened. We were crossing from Europe to USA through the Atlantic, and the ocean was anything but calm.

The waves were raging so violently that a supporting wall for the pool on deck cracked.

The crew was running around in panic, and I was praying, wondering if this was the day. Suddenly, through the ship's announcement system, I heard the captain's voice:

> *"There's a hurricane in our path. The ocean is in a bad mood. We are in God's hands."*

When I heard the captain say, *"We are in God's hands,"* I knew instantly this was the day why I had come to this ship.

I admit, I don't remember whether I went up to the Sky Bar, the highest deck, where waves were crashing against the ship's windows, or whether I stayed near the exit doors on the highest deck. I simply don't recall. What I do remember is that a surge of faith entered me, a conviction to save these people, including Wendy.

I knew nothing would happen to us. After all, God wouldn't give me a future wife just to let us drown in the ocean.

So, for about an hour, I cried out, rebuked the restless waters, and the name of Jesus never left my lips. I prayed as if the lives of many depended on that prayer.

I knocked on heaven's door, pleading with God to change the hurricane's direction and save us.

One hour after the captain's famous words, *"We are in God's hands"*, he came back on the intercom and said: "We are saved. The hurricane has changed direction."

Okay, now you can judge me, but I won't hear you.

I felt as if I had just run a marathon. My eyes were tearing, I was completely drained, mentally, spiritually, physically.

Okay, now you can judge me, but I won't hear you. I felt as if I had just run a marathon. My eyes were tearing, I was completely drained, mentally, spiritually, physically.

The adrenaline had burned through me. You may not believe it, or maybe you will, but your grandpa, your great grandpa, whomever I am to you, the very next day (not a week later, not a month later), walked straight to the Hotel Director. He was either Swiss or Austrian. I said:

"Sir, I'd like to hand in my resignation."

He looked at me as if he'd seen a ghost.

"Excuse me?"

"I'm ending my work on this ship."

He couldn't believe it. *"Why?"*

I told him,

"I've fulfilled my mission. Now I'm stepping onto land to preach the Gospel."

> *"But you can do that here,"* he said. *"Besides, what does 'preach' mean?"*

English wasn't his native language, so I explained that I would be telling people about Jesus, on land.

He couldn't believe it, but he saw there was no point in arguing. I was determined to take this drastic step.

Dear ones, I wasn't on that ship to make money or build a fortune like most of the other crew members.

From the very beginning, I knew why I was there. I had been waiting for the day when my vision would be fulfilled, and the time would come to take the next step in my life.

This time, I wasn't alone, I had a girlfriend. And so it happened. We both disembarked in New York and flew to England to meet Wendy's family.

I laugh when I think of New York. In the hotel bathroom, I was arranging my shaving gear and wondering how to keep it from falling out of the cabinet. Then it hit me, the hotel was firmly planted on solid ground. Nothing should fall out.

I know, I must've seemed crazy. After months in open waters, it had become second nature to think about such things. As the bar manager and wine steward, I had been responsible for securing expensive bottles, so my mind was trained to anticipate motion and instability. I hope you understand me better now. I'm back on land.

The day came when Wendy and I arrived at her hometown. After spending most of my time in sunny parts of the world, I found myself in a land of green fields and nearly constantly drizzling.

The chilly winds weren't exactly something to admire, but what could I do? This was the land where my future wife came from.

Yes, I had serious intentions. Asking Wendy's father for her hand in marriage was no joke.

But in every quiet moment alone with Wendy, I reminded her that Jesus would always be first in my life, and she would be second. In her mind, (these were her own words), she thought:

"How dare he put me second?"

I told her we couldn't be on different spiritual paths; we had to be one in faith. I asked if she was ready to give her life to God.

One day she answered my question positively. We knelt together by the bed, not knowing that her mother was eavesdropping just outside the door. I led Wendy in prayer, laid hands on her to baptize her in the Holy Spirit, and she began to speak timidly in other tongues. And no, there was no earthquake in Somerton, England. A weight fell from my heart. At last, I was spiritually aligned with the woman I loved.

* * * * *

Chapter 13

"Trust In God"
Lucy Mable Wheadon's Testimony

A grandmother's quiet faith that still speaks today.

O NE DAY, WENDY TOOK ME to visit her grandmother, Lucy Mable Wheadon, her father's mother. She lived alone in a small house in a retirement community, where residents had access to medical care and assistance if needed.

While sipping strong English tea with a splash of milk, Wendy turned to her grandmother and said:

> *"You know, Jacek is a very religious person. Please show him what you once wrote."*

I must say, I dislike being called "religious." I took a few handwritten pages from her and began to read what she had written. While Wendy and her grandmother chatted, I finished reading and asked:

> *"Did you share this with the rest of the family?"*

Her grandmother shyly replied:

"No. I thought they'd think I was crazy, a person who believes in Jesus."

My response may not have been polite, but I said:

"That's selfish, not sharing something so important with those who are your family."

To give you a full picture of what I encountered, I'll share what she had written many years ago in its entirety.

(Dear family, Wendy's grandmother is your family too, even if you've never seen or heard of her.)

This is what she wrote, which I later typed up and turned into a video with photos of her and her loved ones. It's your story too, your roots. And to you, dear reader, even if you're not closely related to me, see how God always places someone in the family who prays for the next generations, so that no one is lost, and everyone comes to know Him.

"Trust in God"

by Lucy Mable Wheadon (1992)

Some time ago, I was deeply moved when watching a play on television. It was about a young girl called Bernadette who claimed to have seen a vision of the Virgin Mary.

Since then, I've often felt an urge to tell of a similar experience I had about 12 years ago, but somehow, I could never talk about it, because I felt no one would believe me, that I should be laughed at.

There are several reasons why I feel I should like to write this. To begin, I have a strange feeling that God wishes me to do so.

Chapter 13 - "Trust in God"

Another thing, I hope that by telling this some of my own thoughts, doubts and beliefs of the past three years, I might be able to make someone else understand. I know it will not be easy, but at least I shall have had the satisfaction of knowing that I have tried.

I had always been brought up to believe in God. I was sent to Sunday school and then church. I got confirmed at the age of 14 and continued going to church until I was married, but I did this because it was the usual thing to do, not because it meant anything to me.

I think it was in 1948 that I first realized there was more in it than just going to church and doing what we knew to be right.

I think it was then that some church people came to stay in the village. I went to several of their meetings and thought what good preachers they were, but it meant no more to me until one of them... Sister Birch held a meeting in the Rectory. There was something about her that impressed me more than any preacher ever had before.

I was struck by the light and joy in her face, it convinced me that there truly was something more in what she was saying, though I couldn't quite grasp what it was. I still remember her sermon.

She spoke about the life of the Virgin Mary and two other women. Then she shared how Christ had changed her life, how she had come to know Him as a personal friend, and the joy and happiness that had filled her life ever since. That was something I couldn't understand. For months afterward, she kept coming to mind. Everything she had said in that meeting would return to me, and I kept wondering what she had meant. Around that time, I often felt the urge to go to church.

I hadn't been in years, except for special occasions. I had stopped going when the children came along. Then one Sunday, I decided to go. It wasn't our usual Rector, but a visiting NYLC Evangelist. (National Young Life Campaign) He also spoke about the difference Christ had made in his life and told stories of many others who had experienced the same.

I believe it was at the end of that same year that I, like most of the village, came down with the flu.

One night, unable to sleep, I lay thinking, and I saw an image of Christ on the cross. It was the same as we always see in Bible picture books, but with one difference:

Large drops of blood were running down His face, where the thorns had pierced His forehead. But He was still alive, not dead. It's hard to explain how I felt. It was a mixture of fear and happiness.

I can't explain the fear, except perhaps it was the thought of death. I don't know why, but from a very young age, I had always found the idea of death terrifying. Since that night, whenever I see a picture of Christ on the cross, I still see Him as I did then. Blood running down His face, and that sad, wounded expression in His eyes. I couldn't help but feel how deeply He was suffering. I think it was then that I truly understood the meaning behind the words:

"He died that we might be forgiven."

I knew then, as I had never known before, that it's useless to try to deceive Him. He sees us as we truly are. And at the same time, I knew I no longer needed to fear death. I felt certain that the quiet peace and happiness I experienced at that moment was something I could always carry with me.

I won't pretend that I immediately began reading the Bible or kneeling down to pray. But I did find myself thinking about God more than I ever had before.

As I went about my work, I felt certain He knew everything I was thinking, both good and bad.

Over the next few months, I could hardly understand myself. My entire outlook on life was changing.

I began to see things in a new light. I started going to church again, not out of obligation, but because I genuinely wanted to.

The words of hymns and prayers took on new meaning. I could read a chapter in the Bible without thinking, as I used to,

"There's plenty of time for that when I'm older."

I began to understand what Sister Birch meant when she spoke of Christ as someone she knew personally. I was beginning to feel the same. I no longer thought of God as someone far off in the sky, whom we would meet only when we got old and died, as I had believed since childhood.

Instead, I saw Him as someone alive, and real. I hadn't felt that way until I heard Sister Birch preach. I can't explain what moved me, but something did.

I suppose I was like most people. I believed all the stories we were taught about Christ's life on earth, but no preacher had ever made me feel, as she did, that Christ is alive today, just as much as He was nearly 2,000 years ago, ready to help and guide any of us, if only we ask.

At the end of the Church Army campaign, the Rector continued with weekly meetings at the rectory, which we all enjoyed very much.

Then one evening, he asked us to speak or write about what religion meant to us. I tried several times to write how I felt, but I could never find the right words. Then one day, without any difficulty, I wrote this piece of poetry:

"Grieve Not for Me"
by Lucy Mable Wheadon

Grieve not for me, when from this world I'm gone, for
I shall be going to my Father's home.

I know there is a place there prepared for me, where I can watch and wait for thee.

Twice I have been told that I've nearly gone on that long journey to the great beyond.

But God reads our hearts, and He knew that I was a sinner and not ready to die. Scarcely a thought I gave to Him, just going through life for pleasure and sin.

Only in danger did I think of prayer even then, I seldom thanked Him for all His care. Many of us think there's plenty of time to consider religion and things of that kind. But that, I found out for myself, was quite wrong. We need to begin when we're really quite young.

For none of us know when our time might come to begin our journey to the Heavenly Home.

So, let's begin right now, as we go through life's way, to spare a few moments for God every day.

He is always beside us, so there's no need to say, "I'm ever so busy, and there's no time to pray."

Just tell Him our troubles as we go about our work. He understands, for our thoughts, He can read like a book.

We can't all be preachers if we're not gifted that way. But there are plenty of things we can do in other ways. Just a kind word to others, a helping hand.

And let's speak a word for God whenever we can. Now I'd like to tell you about a wonderful thing that happened to me.

It was back in the spring. As I sat quietly thinking one day, I knew, Christ had entered my heart to stay.

Believe me, dear friends, there's no joy to compare, to the joy you feel when He's dwelling there.

CHAPTER 13 - "TRUST IN GOD"

So do not delay. If you're not trusting in Him, open your heart and let Him come in.

* * *

No one could have been more surprised than I was. I had never written anything like that before, or since. It was as if my own thoughts had been expressed to me. I realized then that God truly helps us. If you're sincere in what you want to say or do, you can do it.

As time went on, I felt more and more that I wanted to share my feelings with my family and others. But I could never bring myself to do it. It takes courage to admit that you believe in God. I found that religion is a bit like politics, it can easily lead to an argument.

I remember clearly reading that poem to my children and telling them I had written it. My eldest son was about twelve at the time. I can still see his serious face as he looked at me and said:

"It's very nice, Mum. But I don't think you wrote it. You must have copied it from a book."

Many things hit home at that moment. He made me realize I was a poor example of what I had written. I knew that many things I told them not to say or do were things I often said and did myself. I also realized that no matter how much we change inwardly, others still judge us by what we say and do.

I know all too well, it's not easy to break the bad habits we've picked up over a lifetime.

I've always been interested in hearing others' opinions about religion and the existence of God. But after these past three years, no one will ever convince me that God doesn't exist.

It was during my illness, just three years ago, that I discovered the true meaning of prayer and faith in God. When I woke from my first real sleep after three weeks of battling faintness and unconsciousness, I couldn't understand why I felt that God had saved me for something.

At the time, I was too weary to care. All I wanted was to sleep. Both doctors said I was worrying about something, though I denied it. I suppose, in a way, they were right. So much passed through my mind as I lay there thinking.

I had never cared much about what others felt. But at that moment, when I thought, I was going to die, it suddenly seemed so important that I said something to my family.

I longed so deeply to share the quiet happiness I had known since that night I saw Christ on the cross. I wanted to tell my family to give more thought to God, to be prepared for whatever life might bring. But I couldn't find the words.

I'll never forget the morning I finally got out of bed. I felt so sick, and waves of faintness kept washing over me. I knew I couldn't fight much longer. Then the thought of my husband and two sons left without anyone to care for them, it was more than I could bear. I broke down and cried. And then I prayed as I had never prayed before, begging for strength to fight the awful weakness that had overtaken me.

I remembered the doctor was coming again that afternoon. No doctor could have been kinder than he had been over the past week.

Yet I couldn't forget that, at the beginning, he had said I was simply giving in to nerves. I wondered if he still thought that.

He had no idea how deeply that hurt.

Nor did he know that, if anything could stir me, usually it was my temper, it was being accused of something I knew wasn't true.

I felt I had to prove to him that I wasn't giving in to nerves. But how could I? I could barely stand on my own, and I was growing weaker by the hour.

Then suddenly, I thought: God had answered my prayers before, why should I doubt Him now?

> *"If I can get downstairs before the doctor arrives,"*

I told myself,

> *"He'll know I'm not giving in to nerves."*

And in trying to prove something to him, I proved something far greater to myself, the power of faith in God. With help, I did get up.

But those first two or three months were a long nightmare. I lived in a kind of trance. Nothing felt real.

I knew there were moments when I was as close to collapse as I had been when I first gave in. But I was determined not to surrender again.

So many things happened in those early weeks, things that couldn't simply be dismissed as fate or coincidence. If I had ever doubted God, I would have had to admit that something was guiding and encouraging me.

At the time, unable to do much work, television became my main source of engagement. Not just for entertainment, but for the serious programs as well. I can honestly say I learned more and gained a deeper understanding of what truly matters in life than I ever had before.

There was one program that helped me especially. It was called Meeting Point, where people from all walks of life came together to talk about religion. Several shared stories of events in their lives that had led them to believe in the existence of God.

One young man in particular caught my attention. He had been suffering from a serious lung condition. By the time the specialist discovered what was wrong, it was too late to treat it. He was told; he had no more than three months to live. Then he said:

> *"Someone told me that God could heal me, if only I would believe and pray for it to happen."*

He continued:

> *"It took me a little while to believe, but once I did, my lungs began to heal. I made a rapid recovery, and within six months, I was in the army doing my national service."*

Listening to that young man made me think of Mr. Jim Wilson, who once gave us a lecture on prayer and faith healing. He spoke about the work being done in London, where clergy and doctors worked together to help people who were seriously ill. He shared many cases, some involving incurable diseases, that had been healed through prayer and faith in God.

I also remembered our former rector, who later started a weekly prayer meeting here. At the time, I refused to join because I thought it was a mockery. I never doubted that God answers prayer. I had seen that proven time and again.

But I struggled to believe that people whom doctors had given up on, those beyond medical help, could be healed by prayer and faith alone. After these past three years, I will never again say it couldn't happen. I've discovered how much prayer can help us in our daily lives, and I sincerely believe that with God's help, anything is possible.

Somehow, that young man convinced me more than any previous speaker ever had. He made me feel that such things truly could happen.

Perhaps I was more moved because he, and many of the others who spoke, were just ordinary-looking people like me.

At that point, I had been out of bed for six weeks, yet I still felt very weak and unwell.

I often wondered why I wasn't making any progress. But listening to him helped me realize many things. I knew that apart from praying so desperately that morning, I hadn't given God a second thought.

I hadn't even thanked Him for giving me the strength to get up. My thoughts during those weeks had been focused entirely on the doctor.

I was so determined that he wouldn't have a second chance to say I was giving in to nerves.

Yet I'll always be grateful to him, because I know that if he hadn't said that I might never have gotten up again.

As I've already mentioned, I couldn't do much work at the time, so I had plenty of time to think. I began to understand many things that had puzzled me before.

Over the following weeks, I had every reason to believe that what I'd heard was true. From that point on, I began to think and feel differently, and soon, I was able to do my own work again. It was during that time, while I still felt very ill, that the thought first came to me to write this.

At the time, I truly didn't believe I would recover. I thought writing might be one way to let my family know what I wanted to say to them.

Around the same time, I began to notice how often certain phrases kept appearing in church services:

"God is life, if only people would believe it," and
"We are all put on this earth to do something for God."
Also, "God puts thoughts and ideas into our minds for us to follow."

I thought a lot about those words, especially about the strange feeling I'd had when I was so ill.

I wondered if the urge to write this had come from God, because He knew I didn't have the courage to say it out loud.

I also wondered if it was a challenge to me, because when I first heard someone say that prayer had succeeded where medicine and drugs had failed, I laughed and said I didn't believe it.

185

About eighteen months later, I began to feel very ill again, even though I had been so sure I was on the path to full recovery. I was told I had blood disease, cancer, and that nothing could be done. All the old doubts came rushing back. To me, it just didn't make sense.

"Why had God saved me when I was so ill, only to take me now, when I had so much more faith in Him?"

My thoughts returned to those few days, especially that morning when I had prayed so earnestly for the strength to get up. I remembered everything I had said, and I knew, God hadn't failed me. I had failed Him.

I believe God can read all our thoughts. He knew how I felt in that moment, and I believe He gave me those extra months to do something with them. But I had done nothing.

Many times, over the next few weeks, I was tempted to burn this writing. It seemed pointless to continue if I wasn't going to get better. But somehow, I couldn't bring myself to do it.

Feeling as I did then, there were days when I would have welcomed death, if not for the fact that I felt I had so much to live for.

So much had happened in the past eighteen months. Both my sons had married, and I no longer had to worry about them. My daughter had given me my first grandchild. Their weekly visits became something I looked forward to with all my heart. But I must admit, the thought of leaving them all did, at times, make me feel very low.

Then, gradually, the same determination not to give in returned.

I knew my life was in God's hands, and that no medicine or willpower could save me if He chose to take me.

Yet I couldn't help thinking about the many talks I had heard. I felt that if others had fought disease by believing God could heal them, then so could I.

In fact, I think it was the very idea that there was no cure for cancer that gave me the courage not to give up. I thought:

"If I live, it will prove to me, and to others, that God truly exists."

And maybe it would be a small encouragement to people like Mr. Wilson, who had made it their life's work to help others believe. But it was a deeply moving sermon by Dr. Billy Graham that finally convinced me to finish writing this.

In it, he said:

"The trouble with the world today is that people think they can live without God. But that is not true. If we want to live, we must do God's will, not our own."

He also said:

"There wouldn't be nearly as much sickness and disease in the world if people prayed and thought more about God."

Another year has passed since I began writing this. But I only have to look back over the past four years to know he was right.

Although I had believed in God for many years, it was during my illness, and after, that I discovered something I had never truly known before. Faith.

I believe we are all given one chance in life to recognize the existence of God. So, I would like to add one final thought:

Don't be like me, afraid to admit it, just because you think someone might laugh.

There will always be someone nearby ready to criticize. But I've found that believing in God is the one thing that truly makes life worth living. Believe me, you will be rewarded with a quiet peace and lasting happiness.

The thought of death doesn't worry me anymore, though I used to dread the idea of spending weeks in bed waiting for it. But since writing this, even that fear has faded. Now I feel only deep peace and satisfaction, knowing that I've finally done something I felt called to do for a long time.

It's been over thirty years since I first wrote this, but I only recently came across it again. I sat down and read it, and my thoughts flew back over the past year, which hasn't been easy, due to very high blood pressure.

At the time, I was feeling very ill, often wondering how many more days I could hold on. On the bad days, when I felt low, I would read it again. Gradually, that quiet peace of mind returned. I stopped worrying about what might happen. I decided to take each day as it comes, thank God each night for another day, and leave the future in His hands.

And each time I read it, I became more convinced than ever that there was truth in what I had written, and that God truly helps us when we ask.

It was around that time that my granddaughter brought her boyfriend to visit me. He was Polish. They had come to England to be married. She said:

> "He's very religious, Gran. Show him what you wrote years ago."

I'll never forget his reaction after reading it. He stood up and said:

> "You mustn't hide this again. You have to let others read it."

Had he been elderly, I might not have thought much of it.

But coming from a young man in his early twenties, his words made a deep impression on me. Now I understand why he spoke that way. He's now living in Poland, as a preacher.

At the time, his encouragement helped me more than he probably realized. But I also felt guilty. I knew he was right. I had been wrong to keep it to myself all those years. I should have shared it. But not being serious by nature, I doubted anyone who knew me would believe I had written it.

Now I know I'm facing something more serious than high blood pressure. It's a growth, and I've had a stroke. For weeks, I felt very low and unwell. Then a passing remark from the doctor sparked some deeper reflection and renewed my faith in God.

He said:

"You seem to have found new life from somewhere."

I knew it wasn't the tablets that had helped me over the past year. I had to stop taking them, they were making me worse.

For some time now, I've felt that my time on earth is nearly over.

But it doesn't worry me. I know I've found something that brings great comfort. It was a television program.

Every Sunday morning, people from all walks of life would gather and talk about serious illnesses they had faced, and how prayer and belief in God had helped them overcome.

I thought a lot about one man. He said he had malignant growth. He underwent radium treatment, but it didn't work. He knew he had little time left. He said:

"For days, I kept thinking about people who claimed they had been healed through prayer and faith in God."

So, he kept praying. Then one evening, he felt as if someone was near, telling him to try to walk. With great difficulty, he stood up. After that, he walked two or three more steps each day.

Now, he can walk down the road to visit his neighbor. He has great faith now that he will truly recover. And I understand how he feels.

For years, I thought I knew what faith in God meant, but it was nothing compared to what I've learned over the past two years. So many times, during this period, I felt like saying:

> "*I know I'm not getting any better, so I might as well give up.*"

But every time I felt that way, something always seemed to come along to change my mind.

I thought back to all those years ago when I laughed and said I didn't believe it, when I first heard that people, given up by doctors as beyond medical help, could be healed through prayer and faith in God.

Now I firmly believe it can happen. Life for me over the past thirty years has passed much like it does for anyone else. I enjoyed the religious programs on television, but I never went to church. The weekly visits from my growing family were what I lived for. It would take too long to explain why I feel so strongly that God is always near, ready to help and quiet our hearts. I've often heard it said that God works through others to help us understand. I believe that.

I also believe that prayer can help us more than we realize. I don't mean we should always be on our knees. But when life's problems feel too heavy, just ask for His help. Often, the answer will come, and often from someone you'd least expect.

When I think about it now, it almost seems laughable, that something I wrote all those years ago, hoping it might help my family (who until recently knew nothing about it), should reappear now to help me in my old age. But I'm sure it has.

Just recently, I started reading a book called *"Healing the Sick"(T.L. Osborn)*. In it, thousands of people from all over the world shared the same testimony. Something they had suffered from for years was healed through prayer and faith in God.

It was my granddaughter's husband who first made me realize that I might have helped others, if only I had let them read what I wrote. They're here on holiday now, so I'm giving this to them, hoping that being a preacher, he might find something in it that will help them in the work they're doing in Poland.

L.M.Wheadon

Wendy's grandmother lived 98 years, 9 months, and 8 days. A beautiful age. I was grateful to have met her, and even my rough, unpolished English, which may have sounded more like an accusation than a conversation somehow touched her. Today, her entire family knows what happened in her life.

Dear reader, I don't know who you are or what country you're from, but if you've had a similar experience, take to heart what you've just read. Share it with someone next to you, with your family, a colleague at work, or a friend at school. These are not cheap things, as my son Isaac often says. They are the fruit of years of prayer and effort, so that the next generation might come to know the Savior personally.

* * * *

Chapter 14

From Shame To Testimony

The day my father's rejection met my Father's call.

I REMEMBER WENDY'S FAMILY, ESPECIALLY her mother, saying,

"That boyfriend of yours, he talks about Jesus all the time!"

I think they were afraid Wendy had fallen into the trap of some cult and that they'd never see her again! And Wendy's reply, not realizing the weight of her words:

"Mom, he's just going through a phase. It'll pass."

Yes, that must have been interesting. I'm writing this book, still broadcasting Jesus with my whole life. And now even Wendy is evangelizing her loved ones.

But let me get back on track and return to the heart of my story.

After a few weeks in England, we traveled together to Poland, landing in Kraków. I hadn't been there in years. In 1989, communism collapsed, the Berlin Wall fell, and the Soviet Union crumbled like sand slipping through fingers. Times had changed completely.

We took the next train to my hometown of Ostrów Wielkopolski. When we arrived at the train station it was late at night. I didn't want to surprise my parents in the middle of the night after so many years apart. So, to pass the time, we went for coffee at the station bar.

It was Wendy's first time in this part of Europe. She only knew Poland from my stories. I ordered two coffees. It came in a glass on a small plate, with about two centimeters of coffee grounds floating on top, because it was "zalewajka," traditional Polish pour-over coffee - Turkish style. Normal for a Pole, but a shock for an English woman.

In the glass was a small aluminum spoon, and beside it, a few cubes of white sugar. Wendy looked at me and asked: *"What is this?"*

I said: *"It's coffee."*

She replied: *"This is soup, not coffee!"*

And so, for years afterward, whenever guests came to our house, Wendy would ask: *"Do you wish to have instant coffee or soup?"*

Only those who've been to Poland will know what I mean, but that was the beginning of our adventure there.

In the morning, we made our way to my family home, and I introduced Wendy to everyone, my parents, Grandma Wanda, Uncle Stefan and Aunt Helena, and many others I can't even name.

We agreed with my sister Anna that we'd stay with her during our visit and so began our journey in Poland.

Wendy returned to England, and I stayed behind to sort out the paperwork so we could get married there.

But it turned out my life had changed so radically that my closest family looked at me like someone they recognized physically but didn't know what to do with what was coming out of me.

I told everyone what had happened to me.

I can only imagine what people said behind my back, because gossip, let's be honest, is probably a national trait! Just kidding, it happens everywhere in the world. One phrase that gets repeated often is:

> "What will people say?" Yes, "What will people say?"

Everyone worries about being talked about by the neighbors, so you must keep up appearances. But I didn't pay attention to that. I thought it was so foolish it was laughable.

Why should I care about what people say when I know I'm speaking the truth, and I won't back down in front of opinions from people who have no idea what they're talking about?

I became uncomfortable for some. After a few weeks, my father, whom I'd never had a good relationship with, looked at me and said:

> "I'm ashamed to have a son who talks nonsense about Jesus and carries my name."

Let me remind you, my grandfather on my father's side was named Mojsej, (Moses) my father Mojsiejów, (a descendant of Moses) from the eastern borderlands, now called Ukraine. And here I was, with that name, talking like a madman about Jesus of Nazareth.

Well then, *"How could I deny Jesus?"*

How could I say:

> "Dear Dad, you're right. I'll stop talking. I'll shut my mouth, fall in line, and never speak up again."

A spiritual war broke out. You could hang an ax in the air; it was that tense. But maybe I inherited my father's stubbornness. I didn't change my behavior, and I did something that surprised everyone.

I went back to England, estranged from my parents because of Jesus. Only my sister Anna and her husband came to my wedding.

And I, alone and without family, approached Wendy's father and asked:

> "Would you mind if, during the wedding ceremony, I took the name Wheadon? My father is ashamed to have a son who carries his name."

Wendy's father immediately agreed. He couldn't understand how faith in Jesus could cause someone to treat their own child that way.

And so, dear ones, now you know why you don't carry my father's name, but the name of Wendy's father.

I don't apologize for being willing to renounce my lineage, which bears the name of Moses. To this day, I don't know whether it was the Jew from Nazareth, whom many Jews still can't stomach, or the fact that my father is an atheist and couldn't bear to hear his only son speak of miracles that had happened in his life.

For those who don't know me, I want to assure you: after many years, I do speak with my father. My son and daughter have visited him in Poland. He's even met my grandchildren, his great-grandchildren. Time heals wounds.

But I owed you an explanation of why a Polish man carries an English surname. And now you have my story.

After a beautiful wedding and joyful celebration, we set off for a three-month honeymoon, back to Poland. It didn't quite go as planned, Poland, meant to be a place of temporary rest, unexpectedly became our home for over twelve years.

We spent our post-wedding vacation in the Polish mountains, exploring other parts of the country, until the moment came when we had to decide what was next. I came up with the idea of returning to sea for a while, to save up some money and perhaps buy an apartment. This time, it was my idea, not God's! I sent applications to ships sailing the waters of Asia and Australia, because Wendy had already been there, and I longed to see that part of the world.

I was offered a position on a massive ship carrying 4,000 passengers, but Wendy couldn't get on the same vessel, so my plans fell through.

Clearly, God had other plans for me. I started looking for work, just to get going. I didn't know anyone among Christians who believed as I did. Everything felt religious, and I struggled to find my place.

In Poland at that time, the vast majority of people became Roman Catholics immediately after birth through infant baptism. I was one of them, so I can speak from experience.

Eventually, Wendy found work as an English teacher in my hometown, everyone in the 1990s wanted to learn English. Before that, Russian and German were taught in schools. We had to learn Russian to communicate with our "brothers," and German to understand the language of the enemy.

If you're from Russia or Germany, please don't take offense, I'm simply recounting the mindset many Poles had back then.

Of course, Wendy didn't speak Polish, which made her all the more desirable as a teacher of English, especially for young people.

During one of her interviews, I was translating for her. The manager at Empik (a local Community Center) turned to me and asked if I could also teach a beginner's course.

I gave a resounding *"no,"* because I had never studied English formally, not in school, not in any course.

As you know, my English began on my knees, crying out to the Lord with a dictionary, asking Him to give me the language so I could preach His Word across the earth.

But after a few days of persistent nudging, I gave in, especially since we could earn a little money. I started teaching from scratch.

I probably spent more time preparing lessons than my students did learning them!

In addition, I got involved in selling life insurance policies through an Austrian company, WVP in Graz.

At that time, it wasn't legally possible to sign such contracts on Polish soil, so we had to organize bus trips from all over Poland to make it happen outside the country!

You might think that's madness, especially knowing that in 2025, you can probably handle such matters instantly on-line from your smartphone.

But back then, it was unheard of, Poland had only just regained independence from under the rule of our Russian "brother," who was quite the character.

In the meantime, we found our own apartment and moved out of Anna and Tomek's place.

As I mentioned earlier, I became a sheep, maybe not a black one, but certainly one people looked at as if I were a man with a strange affliction.

I talked so much about Jesus that even priests didn't speak of Him as often, or so some people gossiped about me behind my back!

One day, my sister told me that her husband, my brother-in-law, had said that if she ever went crazy like Jacek, he'd divorce her. What could we do but pray for their situation?

I didn't want my closest family to go through such turmoil just because they believed in the Lord Jesus. It was incomprehensible to me.

I could understand if I were encouraging people to commit crimes, but to speak that way about someone proclaiming the Kingdom of God? I couldn't grasp it.

After some time and much prayer, my sister called and asked if I was home, she needed to see me. When she crossed the threshold of our apartment, she began to cry, fell to her knees, and sobbed, asking what she must do to be saved.

In Acts 2:36–38, Peter emphasized the responsibility of the people of Israel for what they had done to Jesus:

> "Let all the house of Israel therefore know certainly that God has made Him both Lord and Christ, this Jesus whom you crucified." Now when they heard this, they were cut to the heart, and said to Peter and the rest of the apostles, "Brothers, what shall we do?" Peter said to them, "Repent, and be baptized, every one of you, in the name of Jesus Christ for the forgiveness of sins, and you will receive the gift of the Holy Spirit."
>
> (WEB, Acts 2:36–38)

So, without delay, I asked her what had happened, surely there would be trouble with her husband. But Anna replied,

> *"I don't care. I had a terrible dream last night in which God showed me hell. I woke up drenched in sweat and knew I had to come to you."*

We laid hands on her and began to pray with her for God's mercy over her life, for repentance, for conversion. All that remained was to baptize her in water.

As you can see, everyone has their own path to truth. It's not always easy, but the most important thing is that we teach the truth, and once we know it, it sets us free.

Our neighbor, the daughter of a police officer, heard that I had experienced some extraordinary things in my life. When she heard my story, she said she knew of people in town who spoke a similar language of faith.

She connected me with them, and they came to check me out, to see who I was and what I preached. After all that, they invited me to share my testimony at the Pentecostal church in Ostrów. I had never preached in a church before, apart from being a member in Falkenberg and later in Uppsala. Outside of those places, I had only ever shared one-on-one, never to a larger group.

Dear friends, from that memorable day in 1991, when I first publicly shared my story of conversion, I have stood behind the pulpit for decades, preaching the Gospel.

And as you can see, I still cannot stop giving my testimony about what the Lord has done in my life.

* * * * *

Chapter 15

The Woman God Sent

When destiny boarded a ship called Seabourn Pride.

I MUST RETURN TO ONE more important story to continue. Every Thursday, our home was visited by many young people. We shared discoveries from the Bible, prayed together, and had a wonderful time of what we Christian's call, "Breaking of Bread."

But I noticed that Wendy wasn't too happy with how things were unfolding, and here begins her short story, which deserves a mention in my book.

What God Has Done in My Life?

by Wendy Wheadon

How did Jesus finally get this stubborn girl's attention?

Well, that's what I would like to briefly share with you. To any of my family, friends, or strangers who may be reading, I want to tell you something powerful and meaningful that completely rocked my world in the most amazing way.

There were times growing up in England, if asked about my religion, my response would have been "Church of England," meaning Anglican. But that was just a formality.

To be honest, I never went to church. Sure, I attended funerals and weddings, but it didn't mean anything to me.

Yes, we had RE (Religious Education) at school, forced on everyone. It wasn't a choice, but I couldn't wait to get out of those classes.

Truthfully, I grew up spiritually ignorant, and that was my own fault. I could have explored more. I could have chosen differently. But the real turning point came in my twenties. If someone asked me:

"Who is God to you? Who is Jesus to you?"

My answer would have been:

"Well, I know God exists, but I'm good enough. I don't need Him."

I thought God was for people who were struggling: drug addicts, alcoholics, terminally ill, or the homeless. But I was fine. I was doing well enough on my own, but over time, I realized that was pride.

Side-note: When God has a plan, He will move mountains to help us see the truth. In my case, that truth came through a young Polish guy I had met while working on cruise ships.

He was the first person who ever shared with me who Jesus really was. He told me about a miraculous encounter he had had with Jesus.

So, imagine this, a Brit and a Polak meeting in the Dominican Republic. If that's not the hand of God, I don't know what is.

I was working as a beauty therapist, an esthetician, cosmetologist, and massage therapist all rolled into one. I'd always had a desire to travel, and that's why I chose that profession. In my mind, I had created this life all by myself.

I had worked hard, knocked on every door, and kept pushing until something opened. I believed I could control my own destiny.

I had no idea God was working behind the scenes. He had a plan. I had completed two nine-month contracts on ships, traveling the world for free, working my way around.

Then, on my third contract, something strange happened. Normally, I'd stay on one ship for the full term. But this time, I was transferred "twice" in one contract, after a month... and then again, another month later... until I landed on a very luxurious ship, called Seabourn Pride.

Back then, one day on that ship cost $1,000. It was classy. One of the first people I met was this Polish guy in the crew mess (canteen). He was polite, kind, but not my type. He decided he wanted to be my friend.

Later, I learned he had been praying for a wife. For years, he didn't want to marry, he was on the ship to share the Gospel with anyone he could. But between contracts, he changed his prayer:

"God, forget that. I need a woman in my life."

He prayed specifically, for someone English-speaking, not too tall... he had a whole list. And low and behold, during that time, I was being transferred from ship to ship.

During my first week or two, there was a crew party on deck. I liked partying, but not to the extent that everyone knew I was the new girl on board!

So, I went to bed. But at midnight, I felt compelled to get dressed and go up to the party. To this day, I don't know if God had sent an angel or what!

I hadn't even reached the top of the stairs when the Polish guy pounced like a lion, sat me down, and told me his whole life story of how he had encountered Jesus. My first thought?

"This guy's in a cult. Run!"

I'd never heard anyone speak so passionately about Jesus. But it was what Jesus had done in him. He had wanted to commit suicide.

He'd reached the end of his prideful life, realizing he couldn't do anything in his own strength.

So, out of desperation, he cried out to God, and Jesus moved in his life. He shared his testimony for four hours!

I was torn, fascinated, but scared. I was 25, and I'd never heard anyone speak like that before. He had learned English from the Bible.

So, when he spoke in his broken English, he used words this pagan girl had never heard before. I felt very ignorant. At the end of the conversation, he said,

> *"If you'd like to be friends please say hello to me tomorrow."*

He was used to being rejected. People mocked him, called him *"Jesus,"* behind his back and ran when they saw him coming. I didn't know any of that, because I was the new girl.

He went back to his cabin and prayed, *"God, is she the one?"* He felt the Holy Spirit say, *"Yes, she's the one."*

Then came the second question: *"But she doesn't know You."*

And again, he felt the Lord say, *"I've put it into your hands."*

Weird? Maybe. But God hears our prayers. Looking back on that time, it was like God gave him supernatural perseverance, because I was nasty to him.

God literally trapped me on that ship. I would have run. He was sweet, but it was *"Jesus"* every other word. I wanted him to shut up and talk about something else. He'd say things like:

> *"Jesus will always be number one in our life if we ever get together."* I thought, *"Jesus, not me??"*

He bought me a gold bracelet and said he was investing in our future—when we weren't even dating!

> *"Where's the vomit bucket?"*

I thought, *"The arrogance!"* He drove me nuts. But again, God trapped me on that tiny 250 passenger ship. I couldn't run.

But God had a plan. What started as a simple friendship, me saying hello the next day, turned into something more.

He worked in the bars, dressed well, but I thought he used too much hairspray, was just too gentle and polite. I actually thought he was gay. *(He's not, and he doesn't like hearing that.)*

He pursued me like a puppy dog with its tail between its legs. It was too much for this Somerset girl. But we spent seven months together on that ship... Whenever I bumped into him, it felt like I was getting yet another Bible lesson. He was so in love with Jesus and grateful for what He had done in his life, that he couldn't speak about anything or anyone else! He'd always share something he had just read, and I'd think,

> *"Yeah, that's cool... but can we talk about something else?"*

Fast forward seven months, and it was as if God had done a heart transplant in me. I went from seeing this guy as just a potential friend, one I could just about tolerate, to falling head over hills in love with. We started talking about marriage; it was a whirlwind romance.

He would often tell me that if we were to get married, we needed to be spiritually aligned. He'd quote the Bible:

> *"There is no fellowship between light and darkness,"*
> explaining that spiritual disunity would be a problem.

That principle went straight over my head. He also said that for us to truly be in agreement, I needed to be "Born Again". I remember thinking:

> *"I don't even know what that means."*

He explained it to me a hundred times, but I wasn't ready to receive it. It's not something you can just check off a list; it's something God has to do within your heart!

He'd check in with me from time to time:

> *"Are you ready?"* And I'd say, *"No, I'm good."*

But God, in His goodness, and this still blows me away, knows us all individually and knows the perfect timing to get our attention. The Bible says:

> "For my thoughts are not your thoughts, and your ways are not my ways," says Yahweh.
>
> (WEB, Isaiah 55:8)

Looking back, I can see how the Lord was gently drawing me to Himself, like weaving a golden thread throughout my life.

One of those moments happened while we were crossing from London to New York. Remember the Seabourn Pride was a small 250 passenger ship, and at times it bounced around like a cork in crazy waves.

Jacek, the Polish guy I'm talking about, had told me that God had placed him on that ship to rebuke a storm, just like in the Bible. I thought, *"That's crazy!"* But I took it for what it was.

Sure enough, we did face a storm. Before it reached its climax, I was in my cabin during lunch break, fiddling with the TV. We were in the middle of nowhere, so there was no reception.

Still, I kept trying, and for about 10 seconds, a preacher appeared on the screen. It was like:

"Wait, someone else talks like Jacek?"

I had always thought he was a bit off, but now there were two people in the world speaking the same way. It was a small confirmation; maybe he's not so wacky after all.

Then the storm hit. *The captain actually said, "We're in God's hands now!"* This is part of Jacek's testimony, but he went up and rebuked the storm.

One hour later, the hurricane had changed direction, and the captain announced the storm had altered its course.

CHAPTER 15 - THE WOMAN GOD SENT

That was a powerful moment, especially for Jacek, since he had been given that assignment. We sailed up the London Thames in the UK, where my family came aboard.

Jacek had prepared a beautiful presentation, of caviar, champagne, and shocked everyone (including myself) by asking my dad for my hand in marriage. My response was, "Well, you could've asked me first!"

But Jacek wanted to do it the proper way, and my family was thrilled.

We left the ship together, completing out contracts in New York, and then spent a month in England before heading to Poland.

Jacek hadn't been back in several years. Communism had fallen, and the country had changed. While in England, Jacek was simply being himself, sharing Jesus with everyone.

I mention this to show how ignorant I was back then. My family was concerned, especially my mum, about his strong belief in God.

She asked:

> *"What about this Jesus thing he keeps talking about? Are you sure about going to Poland?"*

Out of ignorance, I said:

> *"Mum, it's just a phase he's going through."*

That was the worst thing I could've said. Sorry, Mum. I really didn't get it at that time! During that month in England, Jacek said again:

> *"If you're ready, and we're going to be together, we need to get married. But you really need to give your life to Jesus first. Are you ready to pray with me about that?" I said: "yes".*

I was about 25, and it was the first time I had ever prayed like that. He led me through a prayer, and I repeated it.

You sometimes hear about the "sinner's prayer", which I later learned isn't actually in the Bible, but that's another topic.

After praying, I didn't know what to expect. I thought maybe the earth would shake or lightning would strike. But nothing happened. It was painless. I wondered why it had taken me so long.

We left England together, and now I could call myself a Born-Again Christian, meaning I had surrendered my life to Jesus and received what He had for me in return. Poland was the beginning of a whole new experience. Jacek hadn't been back since his encounter with Jesus, so when we returned to his hometown, people saw he looked the same, but what came out of his mouth was completely different.

Very quickly, people started swarming around him like bees to honey, wanting to hear what he had to share.

In the meantime, we went back to England to get married, then returned to Poland for what was supposed to be a honeymoon, but it lasted 12 years... a very long honeymoon!

For me, it was a time of many changes, a new family and friends, a different culture, a difficult language, and most challenging, a new spiritual life.

People kept coming to our home, drinking my coffee, eating my cookies, and I was getting madder by the day, and even jealousy was creeping in! I felt like these new visitors were stealing my new husband from me. I had no desire to read the Bible or pray. I just wanted to keep my house clean.

We got married on Jacek's 30th birthday, so we had no excuse for forgetting our anniversary!

That first year of marriage was tough. Lots of head-butting. When we had a heated disagreement Jacek would suggest holding hands to pray. I'm ashamed to say on many of those occasions, I would pull away, shout some obscenity and walk off!

About a year after I had said that initial prayer in England, we had another big argument (one of many), but this time I believe the Holy Spirit used that opportunity to speak a message to me through Jacek.

He said:

> "*You know what your problem is? You never really gave your life to Jesus!!*"

It was a light bulb moment. The truth hit me hard. I hadn't meant to deceive anyone, but I realized I had gone through the motions to receive Jacek in my life and not Jesus.

Spiritually, nothing had changed. It was all head knowledge. I had unintentionally put on a religious mask, pretending everything was fine.

I had added a Christian sticker to my name, and thought I had received my ticket to heaven, but nothing had spiritually changed.

Those words that had come out of Jacek's mouth felt like a knife in my heart. I started crying, bawling, for three hours. I went to the bedroom and just wept. The first thing I said was:

> "*God, I'm sorry. Sorry for deceiving You,*" as if God didn't already know.

But that was the moment I truly asked for forgiveness. There's a word for it: Repentance. It means confessing your wrongdoings, asking God to forgive you, and turning your life around.

That was the beginning of my long road of transformation. I cried and cried; it was such a cleansing. I realized how good and faithful God was and how much He loved us. If anything had happened to me before that moment, I would've been eternally separated from Him. I would have ended up in Hell! God is holy, and sin cannot be in His presence. That moment is when I truly believe I was born from above, adopted into God's family.

That's when everything started to change, 180 degrees. And I'm so grateful no one had told me before about getting baptized in water, because if I had been baptized before I truly understood the Gospel, I would have only attended a pool party and ended up wet!

Yes, I had been sprinkled as an infant in the Anglican Church, but I didn't even know what that meant.

You must be old enough to acknowledge your decision. You can't be a baby. You have to be ready and say:

"I choose to live my life according to God's Word."

Then, upon that confession, you're baptized (immersed completely under water symbolizing the death, burial and resurrection) in obedience to Christ.

From that moment on, my spiritual growth began to accelerate. I now desired to spend time with God in prayer and reading His Word. I longed to be with other disciples of Jesus.

I was hungry to learn more. My adventure with God started that day, and it continues on. At the time of this writing, we've been married for 34 years. If you subtract the year I was *"play acting"* at being a Christian, then I've been walking with God 33 years.

It was the best decision I have ever made. I regret that it took me so long! But the journey isn't over. I truly believe there's so much more to come.

* * *

That was a brief glimpse of what Wendy experienced.

* * * *

Chapter 16

From Wounds To Witness

Pain became the teacher, and forgiveness the graduation.

FOR THOSE WHO DON'T KNOW me: I always wanted to finish agricultural college and pursue a career in food technology. Later, I dreamed of becoming a lawyer. But none of that ever happened. My parents were pragmatic; they taught me to survive and make my way in life despite any obstacles.

But God sent me to His own University of Life, where I studied His Word and fed multitudes, not with food, but with the Bread of Life.

I taught and preached to professors, scholars, and educated minds, me, a master waiter with no formal higher education. I didn't become a lawyer, but for decades I taught law, God's Law. I think it's fair to say that God has a sense of humor.

If He could use the proverbial donkey in the Bible, the one from Balaam's story, then He could use me too. You can read about it in the Book of Numbers, chapter 22, verses 21–33.

The donkey spoke with a human voice, warning the prophet of danger and of the angel with a sword standing in the road.

It's the only instance in the Bible where an animal speaks to a human. I write this so that you, dear reader, will remember, engrave it in your heart, that with God, you can do all things to expand His Kingdom.

I even became an ambassador of the Kingdom of God. You may laugh, stomp your feet, and say you don't see or hear it, but these are the roles God gives to those who seek His Kingdom first.

You too can take to heart the title of this book:

"You Are Loved and You are Needed"

But only you can respond to that call and accept it.

Let me mention a few more things before I close this book. I know that in today's world, people don't have much time to read, unless they're truly searching for something that can pull them out of the madness surrounding them.

Walking through the streets of Ostrów, which had once again become my home, I suddenly remembered things that happened over twenty years ago when I was a young boy attending religious classes. Everyone had to go, otherwise, what would people say?

So, families sent their children to religion classes, which at that time were held outside of school hours.

In Ostrów Wielkopolski, there was, and still is, a small church, as we used to call it. Across the street was a Primary School No. 4, which, according to what people said, had once been a Jewish school. But when you're not even nine years old, history doesn't matter.

Suddenly, after two decades, images came flooding back. I don't know how they surfaced, but they did. After one of those religion classes, I was invited by the priest, a handsome man with curly black hair, around 40–45 years old, if memory serves, to help make attendance cards. I would pierce intersecting lines with a needle, punching through several sheets, and then, using a ruler, I'd draw lines with a pencil or pen to create columns for the priest's records.

And now comes a part that isn't very pretty.

The priest I trusted would sit me on his lap. I would draw the lines from hole to hole, while he held a brandy snifter in one hand, warming it with his palm to release the bouquet of the liquor.

At the time I didn't understand what that meant. With his other hand he reached where no child should ever be touched.

Why do I write this? How dare I raise something so painful? I do it for you, dear reader, so you know that among the sheep there are wolves in sheep's clothing.

Not everyone who wears a cassock or speaks about God belongs to Him. They are not friends. They are enemies straight from hell, who destroy the innocent lives of young people. I didn't read this in any book or newspaper. I lived it.

But today I know one thing, God was there with me then.

Not to cause it, but so that one day He could turn my pain into a testimony that would touch others.

He saw everything. And although I was silent for years, He never stopped speaking to my heart:

"Do not be afraid of the truth. Through it comes healing."

I searched for a photo of that priest from around 1968–1971, but I never found one. I still remember his face to this day. He is probably dead by now. I wanted to find him, at first I thought I would beat him up, you know what I mean.

But then I wanted to forgive him, hoping that he had stopped and never hurt anyone again. It never occurred to me to go to the police.

But for you, dear reader, I want you to remember what I'm about to say. It is your duty to teach your children what you believe. Never, I repeat, never delegate that responsibility to strangers. It is your sacred obligation to raise the next generation by teaching them what is written in the Word of God.

Do not destroy your children, your own offspring, by trusting that someone else cares about them as much as you do. That is a lie straight from the pit of hell.

My father is 88 years old in 2025, and I'm sure when he reads what I've written here, his blood pressure will spike, I can almost hear him already. But I forgave that priest.

I understand now that he was trapped in a human tradition that never should have condemned healthy men or women to such torment, forcing them to suppress their God-given sexual nature while still in full reproductive health.

God created us to multiply, not to build sick institutions that have no foundation in His Word. Maybe I'll write more about that in the next book.

Let me return to the story after that drastic digression.

A few weeks later, I received a phone call from someone who had attended the same Bible school as I did. He invited me to a New Year's conference. While traveling by train, I stood in the corridor by the window, holding the window latch, when suddenly I heard a familiar voice: "This will be your next place." I turned to Wendy and said quietly:

"I just heard the Lord say He's sending us to this city."

Back then, in 1992, the city had half a million residents. Wendy replied:

"After living in Ostrów with 70,000 people, I've always wanted to live in a small town."

I laughed because she didn't realize that Szczecin is a large Polish city. And so it happened. Six months later, we moved there.

On the day of the move, while driving with all our belongings in the car, I was told that that evening I would be leading either a youth meeting or a men's gathering.

I was driving my Subaru Libero, having no idea where we were even going to live. The pastor of the local church rented us an apartment, which I had to pay for in German marks. He had assumed that since my wife was English, we would be sleeping on pillows stuffed with money. I wanted to turn back to Ostrów before we even arrived.

But Wendy reminded me of what the Lord had said, and that the devil would do everything he could to discourage me from fulfilling what God had prepared.

I taught at a small Bible school there, evangelism and beginner English. Wendy also taught English at the bible school. But the finances were very tight, so I continued working in insurance to make ends meet.

One day, we organized another trip to the Czech Republic to sign people up for life insurance policies. During that trip, a high-ranking figure from the insurance company asked me to give a motivational speech to the people in the hall.

I don't remember how many were there, maybe 100, 150, or even 200. After my speech, that executive approached me and offered me a position in Warsaw as Director of Human Resources, for ten times my current salary. Years later, I realized that wasn't normal.

Today I know it was a demonic attempt to bribe me in the time of need, to pull me away from the city to which God had sent me. When I returned to Wendy and told her about the offer, she was excited at the mention of Warsaw. But I said:

> "After praying and crying out to the Lord, I've decided to reject it. Even though it would solve our financial problems, but the Lord sent me to this city, I won't

> *deviate from His path. I don't yet know what He has for me here, but Warsaw is not the answer."*

Dear friends, you have no idea how poor we were. In the evenings, we'd go for walks and pass by a newspaper kiosk. Behind the glass were delicious Polish chocolates. We couldn't even afford one. When I asked the pastor for money at the end of the month, he'd reply:

> *"You only ever talk about money."*

So we worked, we prayed, and we tried to overcome every obstacle, because we knew the Lord had something for us, even if we didn't yet know what it was.

When our fridge was down to just the metal racks, no food at all, we walked to Turzyn, a market where you could buy things cheaper than in the stores. After praying, Artur J. knocked on our door. Shyly, he handed us a plastic bag with a piece of pork fat and a green leek. He said:

> *"I don't know what's going on, but I prayed and brought you what I could afford."*

He didn't know that behind the nice clothes, the car, and our clean appearance, we had no money, because the pastor wasn't paying us.

We never told him any of this. I fell to my knees and cried out to the Lord:

> *"God, You sent me here, and I don't understand why it's so hard. I don't have money for rent. We don't even have anyone to borrow from; Wendy's family are ordinary people, and they're not swimming in money either."*

Maybe an hour later, the phone rang. It was Margit from Uppsala, Sweden. She said some money had arrived for me and asked what she should do with it. Dear reader, when trouble comes, we turn to God. We were in desperate need of a miracle.

We were both working, we weren't lying around doing nothing. But someone had misled us, pulled the wool over our eyes. I don't know if it was part of God's plan or if He simply used it to show us that He was watching over us. I was reminded of a verse:

> "For you, God, have tested us. You have refined us, as silver is refined." (WEB, Psalm 66:10)

God examines and purifies our inner being like a silversmith refining silver in fire. He allows His servants to go through trials to remove every impurity. I could have given up and said:

> *"Lord, I have a wife, I serve You, the one and only living God, and yet I can't even afford a simple bar of chocolate."*

Beloved, remember this: God sees how we behave when we have no money, and He watches us just as closely when we do.

Money is nothing more than a magnifying glass, it reveals who we truly are, both to ourselves and to others.

It's like a tube of tooth paste. Next time you brush your teeth, notice what happens.

You don't think about it, but the contents only come out when you apply pressure. That's when you see the toothpaste. Life is the same. Hard times reveal who we are when the pressure of fear and uncertainty squeezes us more than we ever expected.

Speaking of the silversmith, do you know how long he refines silver? He sits and watches as the impurities rise to the surface.

He stays by the vessel, carefully observing and skimming off the dross until he sees his own reflection in the silver. Only then does he know it's pure. That's a lot to think about. So instead of rebelling or throwing in the towel as a sign of surrender, do what we did: fall to your knees, fall on your face, and cry out to the Lord for help.

Remember, the season of refining, the removal of dross, is simply a stage in your walk with the Lord.

No one can skip this stage. Absolutely everyone must go through it, or they'll fall away.

To close, I want to share something I noticed in the Book of Exodus:

> "Sanctify to me all of the firstborn, whatever opens the womb among the children of Israel, both of man and of animal. It is mine." (WEB, Exodus 13:2)

Years later, I discovered that I was the first grandson of my grandmother Wanda. She lost her husband in the labor camp at Rogoźnica, Gross-Rosen, starved to death by the Nazi Germany. She had only one daughter, and of all her grandchildren, I was the oldest. Based on that verse, it's no wonder that God lays claim to the firstborn.

"He belongs to Him".

When I wrote this final part, Wendy asked if it was really necessary. I prayed about it and received confirmation that I should leave it as it is. I don't know who you are, dear reader, but I can see that this is meant to be served to you on this book's plate, so that perhaps you might reflect on it more deeply.

* * * * *

Chapter 17

"Don't Waste Your Last Breath"

*I thought I had already said everything
I wanted to say in this book.*

BUT WHEN I GATHERED IT all together, something still felt incomplete. It wasn't finished. And then it came before my eyes, the same thing I always tell people when I share the story of my life.

Go into a room. Close the door if you can. Don't take your phone, don't take your iPad, just you, and nothing else. Sit comfortably in a chair. Close your eyes. Let nothing distract you. Take off that outer mask number 48, the one that says... *"Everything's fine, I'm strong, I've got it all under control."*

And start talking to the One who knows you through and through. You can't hide anything from Him. Absolutely nothing. Tell Him what's eating you inside, because our conscience is something invisible, but it can sting and burn. If you need to cry out in anger, helplessness, or despair, do it!

And say:

"God, if You really exist, please, help me. I read the book written by that former waiter, he has no idea how deeply his words touched me.

I don't want to be mistaken about my life, the life You gave to my parents, and through them, to me. It doesn't matter who they were, without Your will, I wouldn't be here.

Please, help me in my weakness. I want to find that treasure the author writes about. You have engraved something on his soul, an invisible tattoo that the spiritual world can see, showing he belongs to You.

I have never read the Bible, just like he hadn't at first, but I don't want to end up in some dead religion. I'm tired of staring at carved idols. If You truly are the Risen Savior, please, let me know You.

I want my wife and my children to be proud of me. I want the courage to tell my family and coworkers that I have believed, and that I am not ashamed.

I don't want to live by the slogan, "What will people think?"

I want to be able to say, like Jack, "Lord, what will You say about how I lived, and whether I listened to Your voice?"

I want to teach my children what I believe and whom I follow.

I want my son and daughter to be proud of my courage, that Your opinion means more to me than the opinion of this world, a world that exists today and disappears tomorrow.

Help me escape the snares of this world. Cut off the millstone hanging around my neck, which is crushing my soul every day through my sinful deeds.

Teach me to forgive those who have hurt me.

I don't want to mindlessly repeat memorized prayers and phrases. I want my heart to burst with worship and gratitude for what You have done, and will still do for me.

Renew my mind, wash it in the cleansing bath of Your Word. Show me that You are the Holy God, before whom every knee will bow and every tongue confess that Jesus Christ is Lord and Savior.

Please help me see that God the Father is holy, and that sin cannot stand in His presence. Please reveal to me why a perfect sacrifice had to be made for my sins by You, Jesus.

I beg You, give me a vision, a dream, a word, a warning, anything. I am open to Your intervention!"

* * *

I believe that such a heart, such a cry, shows God that you stand at the door of your life and open it wide, inviting Him in, to dine with you, and to transform your entire sinful life.

He will forgive you when He sees your humility and your awareness of who you are. It is possible. It is real. And it happened in my sinful life.

You've seen me on the pages of this book, wandering the highways of Copenhagen, ready to end my life.

Let me ask you one last question.

"If I saw you in that same situation, how much hatred would I have to carry in my heart to let you throw yourself under the wheels of an oncoming truck without try-

ing to stop you? How much hatred would it take to let you die like that?"

If I ran and pushed you away from that truck, would you see it as aggression, or as love? Would you understand that I only wanted to save you from an approaching tragedy?

Believe me, I too was a lost man. I adopted that attitude from the person closest to me, my own parent. He wasn't famous, didn't write books, or make movies, so I won't quote him, but I will show you a few great people of this world, who, like every living creature, died.

Please, have the courage to read not what they said a month before their death, not a week before, but what they said in their last breath, yes, in the very moment they gave up their spirit.

You are not merely a body that dies.

You are a spirit living within this body, and you have a soul.

I am only a very simple man explaining this to you, but I beg you, these are the final words of this book. Read them carefully.

Throughout history, many great thinkers, rulers, and writers, people admired for their intelligence, power, or creativity, faced their final moments with very different realizations.

Some had mocked faith in God during their lives, others sought truth only at the end.

Listen to their final words:

Voltaire, one of France's most famous philosophers and outspoken critics of Christianity. As he lay dying, he reportedly cried, "I am abandoned by God and man. I am going to hell."

Thomas Paine, the English born writer who helped inspire the American Revolution and wrote The Age of Reason to attack organized religion. Near death he lamented, "I would give worlds, if I had them, that The Age of Reason had never been published."

Sir Francis Newport, a wealthy English nobleman and skeptic who led a club devoted to denying God. On his deathbed he cried out, "Oh eternity. Eternity. Nothing for me but hell."

David Hume, a Scottish philosopher who denied the existence of miracles and questioned faith. His nurse said he died in deep despair, "It was a horrifying sight."

Thomas Hobbes, an English thinker who believed life was driven by fear and power, not by God. As death approached, he said, "I am about to take a fearful leap into the dark."

César de Borja, a powerful Italian politician and soldier, known for his ruthless ambition. When death came suddenly, he admitted, "In my life I provided for everything, except death. Now I must die, and I am unprepared."

Anthony Flew, once one of the world's leading atheist philosophers, who later renounced atheism, saying near the end of his life, "Now I believe in God."

Aldous Huxley, the British author of Brave New World, who explored both science and mysticism. On his deathbed, he requested LSD to ease his passing, but also sought spiritual peace.

Napoleon Bonaparte, the great French emperor and conqueror. Reflecting on his life and power, he confessed, *"I know men, and I tell you, Jesus Christ was no mere man."*

Their final words remind us that intellect, fame, and power cannot answer the most important question of all:

Where will your soul go when your body dies?

>This is not a sentence.

>This is not an accusation.

>This is my outstretched hand.

If you are still breathing, it means God is giving you time. And I, a simple man who was once a fool, ask you:

Don't waste your last breath. Don't wait until it's too late. Don't postpone that decision for "someday," because "someday" may never come.

You don't have to be a theologian. You don't have to know all the answers. But you can say today: "Jesus, if You are real, show me

the truth. I don't want to die in darkness. I don't want to leap into the abyss without hope.

You don't need to understand everything, but you can start with one step, with one whisper of the heart that God hears louder than the roar of a crowd.

He saved me, a man who wanted to die on the streets of Copenhagen, then He can save anyone... Even you!

I'm only a road sign pointing you toward the treasure.

You must find it!

Dig it up for yourself!

Value it.

Possess it!

Let this be your moment.

Let this be your chapter,

**one that doesn't end
with this book,**

but begins in your life.

* * * * *

I Have A Small Request

If you believe this story should be passed on, then the next time you go out to dinner at a restaurant, pray that the Holy Spirit will guide you, and give a copy of this book to the waiter or waitress who serves you.

Let my story become a tool in your hands to show those who already serve at your table that perhaps they are called to serve at the Lord's table. And if you happen to have more money than you need, I ask you: go to a bookstore and buy the best Bible you can find. Make it a gift for your server. That book changed my life, and through me, it has changed many others who now serve God in different countries around the world.

And if you didn't quite finish reading it, then I have no choice but to cry out to the Lord, asking Him to help you finish reading this book, so that the Holy Spirit may touch you as He touched me, and that your name too may be written in the Book of Life, if it is not written there yet.

Until we speak again, or meet again, and if I am no longer among you, know this: I am still alive. My body may have died, but I've simply changed my address. Have I gone mad?

No, I believe in God's Word. And here it is, Jesus said:

"I am the source of resurrection and life. Whoever trusts in Me will live, even after death. And anyone who lives and believes will never truly die. Do you believe this?"

> May God bless you in the powerful Name
> of Jesus of Nazareth, the Lord of lords
> and King of kings.

Jack Wheadon (Jacek)

* * * * *

Notes & References

All Scripture quotations are taken from the World English Bible (WEB), a public-domain translation. No other Bible versions have been used in this work. Where applicable, verses may be paraphrased or adapted for clarity and emotional expression, while remaining faithful to the original meaning.

Historical statements, reflections, and deathbed quotations cited in this book come from a variety of public-domain sources and traditional accounts. Collections such as Famous Last Words of Saints and Sinners (1949), biographical memoirs, and historical records have preserved many of these testimonies. Their exact wording may vary among editions or translations, but the spirit of each account remains unchanged.

This book is not intended as an academic study but as a personal testimony of faith, written to inspire reflection and hope in the reader's heart. All historical and scriptural references are presented in that spirit.

* * * *

About The Author

Jack Wheadon lives in Arizona with his wife Wendy, with whom he forms a close and united team in life, faith, and service. Their shared journey has taken them through many countries, relocations, experiences, and encounters, and each of these events has left a lasting imprint on the way he views the world. Although he was born in Poland, life led him to Norway, Sweden, England, Western Europe, and the United States. In each of these places, God opened new doors before him, tracing a path he could never have planned on his own.

For many years, Jack has shared his testimony of faith along with personal stories that inspire reflection, hope, and spiritual transformation. He does not speak as a theologian, but as a witness, a man who has gone through deep falls, miraculous deliverances, and quiet moments when God spoke in a gentle voice. His accounts are sincere, stripped down, and often direct, because Jack believes that truth does not need to be embellished.

His writing combines elements of a personal journal, testimony, autobiography, and cultural narrative, creating a bridge between generations, languages, and life experiences. Jack is not afraid to address difficult topics, mistakes, fears, crises, spiritual struggles, and turning points that have shaped his life. At the same time, he knows how to weave these experiences with humor, self irony, and lightness, making his work accessible and close to the reader.

In 2015, he suffered a severe heart attack, and in 2020, he was hospitalized with bilateral pneumonia, most likely caused by Covid-19.

In the face of these experiences, he said,

"and I simply cannot die without leaving these events to my family, my friends, and the rest of the world."

These words became an even stronger motivation for him to write and to share the testimony of a life transformed by grace.

As a writer and a witness of faith, Jack places great importance on authenticity and clarity of message.

He translates his books into multiple languages in order to reach readers around the world. His goal is not to win literary awards, but to touch hearts. Every book he writes is an invitation to sincere reflection, inner dialogue, and spiritual awakening.

At the center of his work is a simple yet profoundly powerful message, "Every person is loved and is needed." These words, heard in the darkest moment of his life, became the foundation of his path and ultimately the title of his book.

Jack writes to leave behind a lasting legacy, the testimony of a life transformed by grace. He hopes that his words will be a light for future generations, for those who one day will seek hope in the midst of their own dark moments. He believes that stories, even the quietest ones, have the power to touch hearts and open eyes.

Today, living in Arizona with Wendy, Jack continues his mission. He prays, he writes, he speaks with people, and he shares his testimony. And above all, he thanks God for every new day in which he can remind someone,

"You are not forgotten.
You are loved. You are needed."

* * * * *

Made in the USA
Coppell, TX
17 February 2026

71594036R00144